God Moves Mountains

One Pebble at a Time

The Healing Journey of
Naomi Stoltzfus

as told to

Linda S. Ingham

God Moves Mountains
One Pebble at a Time

Library of Congress Control Number: 2005922275

International Standard Book Number: 1-9-32864-22-9

Masthof Press
219 Mill Road
Morgantown, PA 19543-9516

Contents

Dedication

      I dedicate this book to my beloved husband, David, from whom I have learned the humble ministry of Jesus. And to our children, John Lee, Nathaniel David, Matthew Ben, and Minerva Grace, from whom I have received unconditional love. Lastly, to our precious grandchildren whom I pray come to know Jesus in a deeper way than I know Him.

Acknowledgements

I promised God that if He would heal me, I would have my life story written in book form. As I have determined to keep that promise, it has been thrilling to watch God cause my dream to be fulfilled.

In sharing the shortcomings of my parents as the story of my life unfolds, it is not my intention to bring any condemnation to them. Every person on this earth is born into a fallen world of sin. In this fallen world we hurt one another, many times without any intention. I know full well that my parents never intended to hurt me. And I do not want to dishonor them in this book. In fact, I truly honor my parents.

I acknowledge the fact that what I experienced within my family is not necessarily the experience of all Amish families, nor is it representative of the values of the Amish.

I wanted to thank my friends at Wellspring Garden Ministries in standing with me during the journey of seeing my dream fulfilled. Sharon, little did we know during our childhood school days that God would once again entwine our hearts in ministry and during my healing journey. Thank you, Sharon. Miriam, I thank you for your heartfelt compassion. Linda, I thank you for taking the facts of my life and communicating them in such a way that other hurting women can be helped. John Kauffman, I thank you for capturing the message of this book in a picture for the front cover.

- *Naomi Stoltzfus*

Acknowledgements by Author

I thank the Lord for the opportunity of communicating Naomi's life story. It has been very humbling to experience the anointed hand of the Lord shape and mold the message and the fingers of the Lord to move the words where they need to be. I deeply thank the following people for reading the draft manuscript and giving their input.

Naomi's **Amish friends** who gave their blessing. It is primarily for you that Naomi wanted this book to be written.

Dan Beachy, Director and Counselor at Life Ministries, whose humble spirit believes in the power of Naomi's story.

Judy Edinger, Co-founder and Education/Training Coordinator of REST Ministries, whose loving heart and sharp, quick and detailed mind has, for many, many years, always "kept me on my toes."

Diane Fulmer, Naomi's inner healing counselor, whose deep sensitivity ushered in the powerful healing presence of the Holy Spirit during sessions.

Ginny Hammond, my trusted and loyal friend whose loving honesty always takes me where I need to go in the midst of my own journey of healing.

John and Alberta Ingham, my tenderhearted and patient parents whose lifestyle examples mercy coupled with action towards those imprisoned in their pain.

Pastor Titus Kauffman of Petra Christian Fellowship whose insight into the Amish way of life helped to validate the need for this book.

Angela Manley, who steals my heart away as she gave much encouragement while having endured great and deep pain in her own life. May your dream to share your own story in book form be fulfilled!

Elaine Yoder, Counselor at Life Ministries, who taught Naomi much about life and relationships as her first counselor.

I am compelled to acknowledge all of the precious women in prison to whom I have ministered since 1985. As I have listened to your heartbreaking stories, you taught me much about pain, the pain of life that drove you into a darkness extinguishing the light of God's beauty within you and wiping out the magnificent splendor of life. What I have learned from you gave me the ability to take the facts of Naomi's life and communicate them as I have. Thank you so much. May the truths within this book drive you to experience and encounter the outrageous love and breathtaking glory of our Heavenly Father, His Son and His Holy Spirit. I deeply salute you, respect you and honor you. Each one of you is a **beautiful pearl of great price** (Matthew 13:45,46)!

- Linda S. Ingham

Preface

It has been a joy to become Naomi Stoltzfus' friend. During the hours I have spent with Naomi, especially in writing down the facts of her life, I have come to highly respect this woman of silent yet bold strength. Naomi has a courage that rises to the occasion despite the tides raging against her, a determination that soars beyond human expectations, a sensitivity that draws hurting women right into her heart, and an honesty that challenges the superficial. Most precious is her childlike faith and trust in her Lord.

I have no doubt in my mind that Naomi was set apart by God to influence her people, the Old Order Amish, within the realm of life we all experience, that of pain. Although God brought us into relationship with each other through her driving needs, God had a higher plan, a higher purpose: writing a book of her healing journey.

Naomi wanted this book to accomplish four goals: 1) to tell her story; 2) to teach others how to understand the long-term affects of abuse; 3) to help people understand what is involved in the healing journey; and 4) to know that there is help. Yet the overriding message that burned in Naomi's heart and drove her to have this message written in book form, was a passion that her people, the Old Order Amish, learn to understand and deal with their emotions. I have, therefore, attempted to sensitively take Naomi's passion and communicate it in a way that will not only impact her people, but even people outside of her culture. All people need this message.

For those who have been abused and want to read this book, know that you may struggle. As much as you want to read it, you may experience varying types of mental and/or emotional discomfort or pain. You may feel overwhelmed. If that happens, it is okay to put the book down. Talk to a friend and/or write down your thoughts on paper or on the pages of this book. Pick up the book again when you feel safe and stronger. May I suggest that you do not read this book before you go to sleep.

For all who read this book, may you take an honest evaluation of your life and the steps you have taken or need to take to understand and deal with your own pain.

We pray that Naomi's message will help you to meet Jesus Christ at the cross where your pain can be healed, releasing you into the uncontainable and untamable presence of our life-changing Holy Spirit.

Blessings to you!

- Linda S. Ingham

For those who are not familiar with the Old Order Amish way of life, you may want to read Appendix I before reading this book. As you read Appendix I, please know that the Old Order Amish way of life described was Naomi's experience within the Old Order Amish, not necessarily the way of life for all Old Order Amish.

If you desire to learn more about the Amish way of life, you can purchase books that will more thoroughly educate you in this area.

Are You Willing?

How I looked forward to becoming a member of the Amish church! Why? Because my father's **physical beatings** had to stop! And shortly after I became a member, the **sexual abuse** I experienced with one of my father's employees also stopped. Both began when I was in the third grade. Hallelujah, it all finally ended!

Even though, at the age of 16 I freed myself from those confusing and painful events, in reality I continued to *live every single day of my life in the pain of my past*. I had absolutely no idea that the secrets I held inside about my childhood affected my thoughts and feelings in a way that would cause great physical pain and emotional turmoil. In fact, I taught myself how to keep those secrets.

Each memory held inside of me was like a pebble. Because those memories were full of pain, the pebbles had jagged edges instead of being smooth. Those jagged edges produced a pain that caused a deadly poison within me. As those jagged-edged pebbles grew in number during my childhood, they formed into a pile that grew larger and larger.

During my young adult years, that pile grew into a mountain. Although the mountain was invisible to me, it cut off God's precious flow of life within. That mountain made up of jagged-edged pebbles, made daily living hard and anything but great. Shortly after my father's death in March 1977 when I was age 35, that mountain started to crush me because, in reality, I was just a little girl. The pain of deep-rooted anger, fear, shame, and guilt, which daily nourished that mountain, drove me to *welcome death more than life!*

My life was like many lives—full of secrets— secrets that create lies about **God** and **who we really are** as His magnificent creations. Those lies cause us to become spectators living on the outside, watching life go by and wondering why life is better, easier, and certainly more fun for everyone else. And we even become spectators to our own thoughts and feelings, fearful to enter the horrid memories we conveniently tucked away or just left behind. We get stuck in that invisible mountain all by ourselves. We cannot move, let alone bloom and blossom into the person God designed us to be, Many times, we cannot even experience the simple beauty of a pink rose.

I praise God that my mountain was finally moved. But it was moved just one pebble at a time. I believe everyone has a mountain. Some are bigger than others. Whatever the size, it limits or cuts off the beauty and flow of God's life within. He can and will move your mountain, maybe even faster than one pebble at a time!

Are you willing to travel the journey of healing God has for you?

My Childhood Years

September 17, 1942—I was born on that day in Lancaster County, Pennsylvania. My parents were Old Order Amish. I was born the first of six children including three girls and two boys in that order, after me.

Our family was a typical Amish family in that hard work was the priority of each day, except, of course, on Sundays. On school days, I had to be up by 6:00 a.m. to do chores. Because there was so much work, most mornings I felt rushed. I had to do chores after school, too. In our home, unlike other Amish homes, work always came before having fun. I remember going to Ocean City with a friend, but I had to do my chores before leaving. It felt like we could not even have a break for one special day.

My father was an interesting man. At a young age he began to work at a carriage shop learning both the trade and the business. He continued working in this trade as he grew older and after he married my mother. When I was two years old, he started his own carriage shop business and made carriages for our people, the Amish. When I was six years old, we moved several miles into a house that had a large shop behind it. My father needed more space as his business was growing.

Over the years my father became a perfectionist with his trade. The carriages that he made were absolutely beautiful. In fact, he became known all over the United States for his skillful work. In the later years of his life, he also started to restore carriages for many wealthy and famous people in America. I loved my father's shop and I loved being in it. I was so happy when I could help make the carriages. I loved the carriage business more than helping with housework. You might say I was more of a tom-boy and that was certainly frowned upon within the Amish culture.

My earliest memories of life were that of working in my father's shop even before I started attending school. During my school years, I continued to work in my father's shop before and after school. My father taught me how to make mud flaps for the carriages. If they were not perfect, I had to make them over again. I also sanded the carriages. Many times my fingers bled from the coarseness of the sand paper. In addition, I learned how to paint the carriages. I even helped to paint an old carriage that my father was restoring to be used in the Miss America pageant one year. No words can describe the pride I felt in helping with that carriage. Everyday I had to clean each corner of the shop. It had to be perfectly clean. My father would wake me up extra early to clean the shop if I had not cleaned it well enough the day before.

As a child, I learned to become a hard worker and dedicated to any work I did. It was expected. And if those values were not carried out by my father's employees, I would watch him get very frustrated.

I enjoyed the customers and tourists who came to my father's shop because I loved to be around people. In fact, I loved to be around people so much that I made wrong choices. For example, when I knew my father would be away from the shop, I would steal ten cents out of his money box and go to the restaurant down the road. I would buy a big mug of rootbeer and laugh and talk with the people in the restaurant. Life there was simple, pure, full of laughter, and full of fun.

I could not wait to hook up my father's horse and buggy when we would visit friends and family on a Sunday. I loved to cut his hair and I loved watching him play checkers with different men in the community. They played for hours in my father's shop. My father would make popcorn for everyone to eat. He also played the harmonica in a most beautiful way, but he always stopped playing as soon as anyone came into the room. Although my father was a relatively quiet man by nature, he was very friendly. However, I could never understand why he would get angry if my mother invited people over to the house. That never made sense to me.

My father did not spend much time with his family. We would each pray silently at the dinner table before we ate meals. Then, he would eat quickly and either return to his shop or deliver items to other shops. He rarely talked to us at the dinner table. If he did talk, it was only about his business. He also grew very moody and gave everyone the silent treatment when he could not get his own way. A hug was something that we never received. And I never saw my father hug my mother. Unfortunately, loving expression toward his family was something he did not extend.

My father was a very serious man. Laughter was rarely released from his soul. However, I do remember one time when he laughed wholeheartedly from deep within. We were sitting around the table eating supper. We had whipped cream to put on our dessert. It was in a can with a spray nozzle. However, the nozzle would not release the cream. Everyone was trying to make it work, and when it was my turn, I pressed down on the nozzle and the whipped cream suddenly shot out like a loose garden hose creating a messy design all over my father's beard. I never heard our whole family laugh together as heartily as I did that evening. To see my father laugh that hard and loud was a special treat.

My father was a handsome man about six feet tall with black hair. He wore glasses but there were times he also wore contacts. No matter which he wore, his eyes rarely met my eyes. In fact, his eyes were always looking somewhere else. Seeing into my father's soul through his eyes was something I could not do. But I do know that my father listened to me more than my brothers and sisters. Maybe that was because I did so much work for him in his shop.

My father did have some degree of emotional problems because he had an emotional breakdown before he met my mother. But I do not know much about that.

I never really knew my father.

I never really knew my mother either. She was very busy with my three sisters and two brothers who were born after me. When I was young, I remember how she took very good care of our home. Everything had to be perfect. She was a hard worker and made everything clean, neat, and tidy. We did have a very nice home.

As a child, it seemed to me that my mother could do anything. She would sew dresses for all four girls and dress us alike. And she sewed my brothers' clothes, too. Since I did not like to cook and clean, I spent a lot of time in my father's shop instead of learning how to take care of a home. My mother and I did not, therefore, spend much time together. She was very concerned that when the time came for me to get married, I would not be able to make a good meal for my husband. She talked often with me about that.

One thing though that my mother never talked to me about was all the changes that would take place in my body. In looking back, I wish she would have explained some of those things.

As a small child, I thought our home and family was like any other family. I knew no different.

One spring day, when I was nine years old in third grade, it was raining. As my two younger sisters and I were walking home from school, we hopped, skipped, and jumped in puddles along the road, making different kinds and sizes of splashes. Of course, we became very wet. It sure was fun as we tried to run from each other's splashes. We continued to giggle and laugh as we arrived home.

As our mother looked at our wet clothes with great disapproval, each of us immediately remembered the rule—do not jump in puddles. I knew we were in big trouble because mother had given us a final warning several weeks before that day. She said we would be punished if we ever did that again. Anxiety was the theme of supper that evening as I fearfully wondered the outcome of our punishment. In the past, my mother pulled our ears as punishment, but this evening I just knew something more severe was coming.

After supper my mother told me to go out to my father's shop. When I entered the shop, I noticed that my father was holding a tack hammer in his hand. Before I knew it, I was bent over my father's knees. All of a sudden I felt excruciating pain as he struck my lower back over and over with the handle of the tack hammer. I was stunned. I was puzzled. I was confused. I cried. I screamed! As the pain seemed to split my body in two, I kept thinking, "Why was jumping in puddles so bad? When will this stop? God, do I deserve this?" It finally stopped, and I was sent to bed for the night.

Upstairs in my bedroom, I was painfully bewildered about what had happened. I did not understand why my father beat me like he did. Never before had I experienced the horrendous force of an object through my father's hand. In a short while, my sister also came upstairs sobbing from her beating. Then my other sister followed with the same intensity of emotion.

This was new for us. That day began a series of beatings which I experienced throughout my childhood. Unfortunately, beatings actually became an expected part of my childhood even though I did not know why I was beat. Other than that first beating, I only knew one other time, the reason for my beating. One evening, I had accidentally tripped over my aunt while she was doing exercises on the floor of our spare bedroom. In the darkness, I did not see her. Because she thought I did it on purpose, she told my father. The next day I received yet another severe beating. I was not even allowed to explain that it was an accident. There was absolutely no reasoning with my father.

Beatings were always given in my father's carriage shop in front of the tray which held all my father's tools. He would always use the end of his tack hammer which was used to tack carriage upholstery together. When I would enter my father's shop to receive a beating, my steps faltered as every part of my body would shake. I became overwhelmed as a furious fear ravished every single part of my being. My heart raced so fast; I often felt like it was going to come up and out my throat.

My father would say nothing before or after any beating, ad as I already said, he did not tell me why I was receiving a beating or even explain the wrong behavior that I was supposed to have done. And, of course, I would never dare ask. I was not even told to apologize for whatever it was that I supposedly did wrong. On entering my father's shop the next morning, he would avoid me. In fact, no words were ever exchanged between us. After each beating, I would actually experience a brief feeling of relief, only to anticipate and once again feel that heavy anxiety mounting as I waited for the next one. I never knew when I would receive another beating. I cried and screamed during beatings with the hope that my mother would stop them, but she never did. In fact, years later I came to discover that the beatings were usually at her command for something she thought I had done wrong.

That anxiety that seemed to come so faithfully, ripped the joy of life right out of me.

It was good that the beatings were given in the evenings because I could then immediately go to bed and rest. I was so upset after beatings, not only because my body felt the excruciating pain, but because of the humiliation and shame I felt. I did not want to see anyone for fear that they would catch a glimpse of my puffy eyes or notice and question why I was not walking correctly. In fact, for days it was still difficult to walk or sit correctly because of the pain and discomfort in my lower back. Since I had to put my hands behind my back while I was bent over my father's knees, my hands also got beat. So both my buttocks and hands would be black and blue. I can remember how my sisters and I would look at our bruised buttocks in mirrors. It was horrifying.

Unfortunately, telling someone what was happening and how I felt was something I could not and did not do. There was like this silent message within our home that these beatings were never to be shared with anyone else. So I obeyed that silent message.

I was so afraid someone would ask me how my hands got to be black and blue or why I could not walk correctly. Because of that fear, I did a good job of hiding my hands. Neither, did I have any close friends for fear that they would ask me questions. I did, however, listen to the talk of other children to try to find out if they too were beaten. But, I never heard anyone talk about it.

It does amaze me that during those years, no one ever asked me about my bruises or my inability to walk correctly. I now know, however, that people did talk about us and the beatings that we received. Somehow they found out. It is sad that no one ever asked or further inquired about it.

During those times I had bruises, I not only shied away from friends at school, but I also shied away from the customers in my father's shop. Doing that saddened me because as I said earlier, I loved being around the customers. I felt like I was missing out.

For some reason not known to me, I did receive many more beatings than my sisters. We would hear each other screaming, but no one ever stopped them. When the three of us received beatings the same evening, we would tearfully console each other upstairs in our bedroom. How we needed each other as we drew upon each other's strength. Those evenings our world centered on pain. When I think back, it was like having our own little support group.

As time went on, I certainly found myself at different times feeling strong hatred towards my father and mother. I used to wonder, "How could they be so cruel?"

That fall, about six months after the beatings began, and while working in my father's shop, I noticed that there were quite a few people at our house. Our house was right in front of my father's shop. No one would tell me why all those people were there and why I was not allowed to go inside the house. I did know that a doctor was in the house. Then someone told me I had a baby brother. That was a big surprise to me because no one had told me that another baby was coming to our house. I sure was glad that he was a boy because I already had three sisters. At that time I made no connection to what was going on in our home with the birth of my brother. And I had no idea where my new baby brother came from. When my three sisters were born after me, I never even wondered or questioned how they came into existence. But now at the age of nine, I was extremely curious.

There was a nice, young English guy who worked in my father's shop. I knew him because I worked with him. In working with him I knew that he loved to have fun. Because he seemed pretty smart, I curiously asked him how my brother came into being. He did not hesitate to explain sex to me in great detail. And he also talked about other sexual things. I could hardly believe what my ears were hearing. This was all new to me. I never heard anyone talk about these things before that day. So I told no one about our conversation.

The next day I asked him a lot of questions about sex, because I was very curious. And I was very innocent. In the midst of answering my questions, he started to talk sex talk to me. Then he started to fondle me. The first time it happened, I was shocked. I was stunned. I did not know what to do so I just stood frozen in fear while my heart-beat quickly escalated to a high rate as if I had just run ten miles. Out of shear fear my hands moved swiftly, continuing to work while he touched me. I was afraid, but he was the adult. I felt trapped, but he was the adult. I was just nine years old. So I kept working. Working with my hands kept me distracted enough that I did not have to look at him or acknowledge what he was doing.

Somewhere deep inside of me, I knew that what he was doing was wrong. What could or should I do?

However, in the midst of that consuming fear, it was hard to understand the feelings that I felt within my body when he touched me. They were different. They were new. In fact, I found myself actually liking the feelings that I was receiving within my changing body. I could not understand that. How could I feel such dreadful fear, but yet pleasure at the same time? It confused me. I left that day feeling even more bewildered than when I had received the first beating from my father. But because he was the adult and adults held the authority, I guess I was too afraid to say anything to him and certainly too afraid to tell anyone else. So I just worked hard to try to forget about it.

But this behavior continued day after day, month after month, and year after year as I worked in my father's shop. Although there were only two other workers in my father's shop, I often wondered how long this could continue before someone discovered what was happening.

So for me, a day in the life of Naomi Lapp included going to school, doing my chores, working in my father's shop, maybe playing baseball if the weather was nice, getting sexually abused, and some days getting beat. Although those events became normal, I never told anyone about the abuse. I never even told God. In fact, as a child, I never gave God any thought except to question Him during a beating. It just went on and on and on. I had no idea what it was doing to the inside of me. I had no idea that the beauty of life was being stripped away from me.

Shortly after the physical and sexual abuse started, I would vomit every three to four weeks for a couple of days and become extremely weak. My mother took me to the doctor, but he could find nothing wrong. I would drink a lot of cola soda to settle my stomach, but I was relieved when I could eat again. At least I never received beatings during those times of sickness. This cycle of sickness continued until I finished school at the age of 14. But the physical and sexual abuse continued after school was finished.

When I was about 13 years old, I noticed that my mother started to cry a lot. She acted like she was extremely depressed. For a long time, I was even afraid she would hurt herself. Over a period of time, ordinary daily tasks became very hard for her as her depression grew deeper and deeper. There were times she went to her sister's home to just get away and rest.

During those times that my mother was either away or not feeling well, I was in charge of the house. It was a lot of responsibility for me especially because I did not like to do housework. And I did not receive any support from my father because he was rarely at home. For me, it was like being a mother. However, when my mother was well, she actually controlled our home. She made the decisions because my father was hardly ever around. In the midst of the stress in our home, the physical and sexual abuse continued, but I told no one.

In those early teen years, I do remember my father taking me into the living room on the Sundays we did not have church. We only had church every other Sunday. He would force me to memorize Psalm 23 in the German language. I could not understand why none of my brothers and sisters had to memorize these verses. It was just me and my father on those Sundays. I was not comfortable during those times of being alone with my father. Because we had no relationship, I had no desire to do what he wanted me to do. It seemed so dark, cold, and dismal in the living room because my father showed no compassion. And he showed absolutely no interest in me as a person. He did not even explain what Psalm 23 meant to him. He just forced me to memorize the words. Unfortunately, it was only memorized words that flowed off of my tongue. I had no idea what the words were saying to me personally. I learned on those Sundays that my father did not even know me. And he certainly did not know the big secret of what was happening in his shop almost every working day. Little did I know that, on those Sundays, my mind was painting an inaccurate picture of God, certainly with wrong colors.

I was not surprised to find out that my father was not faithful to my mother. Evidently people in town also knew it. I think my mother sensed and suspected his actions long before she found out the truth about his behavior. I believe his behavior contributed to her depression.

Holidays and birthdays were not a special time in our family. Those days were just like any other day. We never celebrated Christmas as Jesus' birthday. In fact, my father was not around much on Christmas Day. As usual, he would just go to his shop. My mother would give me a present wrapped in a store bag usually a couple of weeks before Christmas Day. We went to church at Easter, but we never gave Easter's reason any thought.

I never remember receiving a birthday cake with candles on it. If I did get a present, I usually received it a couple of weeks before my birthday, just like Christmas. I certainly received no attention within my home. But my abuser surely gave me great attention.

We rarely did anything together as a family, although I do remember one time when our family went to the Philadelphia Zoo. My father even came along. That was one of the very few days when we did not have to do chores before leaving. My father hired someone to do them that day. Although many of us got car sick, we had a fun day. I was so glad that we were together as a family. I used to notice how other families spent time together. As I grew older, I no longer felt as if our home and family were like others. I began to feel like every other family had it all together, but we certainly did not! I frequently wondered what was wrong with our family.

I have to admit that my sisters and I had a lot of fun together at various times. Oh yes, sometimes we were ornery with each other. One time, when I was about 14 years old, I had to go to the bathroom after we went to bed. I did not feel like going downstairs, so I decided to open the window in our bedroom and climb out on the porch to go to the bathroom. I figured it was dark and no one would see me going to the bathroom. Well, my sisters locked me out and I could not get back in. I had to be quiet so that my parents would not hear me. After much "silent begging," they finally left me inside.

Many nights we would giggle and giggle before falling asleep. When our father would knock on the stove pipe, however, we knew that we had to be quiet. We had great fun those nights.

Once in awhile, when my father would not be at home for supper, we would have water fights at the supper table. As we threw water on each other from our drinking glasses, our mother just watched. We laughed and had lots of fun. Amazingly, we did not get punished for that. I think our mother had no energy to deal with us sometimes.

My father's father was one of the first Amish to move to Lebanon County, Pennsylvania. Because he lived quite a distance from us, I did not know him well. When I did see him he was very quiet. I never knew his wife, my grandmother, because she died of cancer when I was young. But I did know his second wife a little bit.

It was very different, however, with my mother's parents because we lived near them. My grandmother, however, had a lot of physical problems and she too was depressed. I remember her being like my mother—unable to function. My grandfather was a very funny man who would joke a lot with people. He enjoyed having fun no matter what he was doing.

My grandfather owned and operated a cheese company and feed mill company. After he retired from those businesses, he helped friends start Kitchen Kettle, a tourist area with stores located right in the center of the village of Intercourse. After he retired, he also made carts and chicken coops at his home. We enjoyed spending time with him, because he was a lot of fun. Fun with him seemed to wipe away my anxiety.

My grandfather had ponies and a sleigh, and he would allow me to hitch up the pony and sleigh and ride it through town when the wintry storms arrived. My sisters would jump in the sleigh, and we would pick up other children in town. At night time, we would take flashlights hoping they would provide enough light for us to see. We did not think much about danger. We just had fun! During the Christmas season, we would ride through town on our sleigh, singing *Jingle Bells*, while ringing bells and waving to all of the neighbors.

My grandfather used to make pony carts. During other seasons of the year we would hook up the pony to those carts and ride through town as well. I seemed to become alive as a person on these rides.

I thought my grandfather was a pretty neat man because he trusted me to drive the sleigh and carts. I wonder what he would have thought if he had known that I was sexually abused on a regular basis in my father's shop. Unfortunately, back in those days, this type of behavior was never discussed.

There were a lot of neighborhood children where I lived. My sisters and I each had a dolly, and we would play dollies with our neighbor friends. My sisters played with their dollies much more than I did. I preferred to play baseball because it was a lot more fun. My father allowed us to play baseball in the field behind our home. He would even let us continue to play if we would break a window. Of course, I would always have to clean up the broken glass. It was absolutely amazing to me that I did not get beat when the windows were broken.

I loved everything about school except arithmetic. Recess was a favorite time because I could play baseball. There was only one other girl who also enjoyed playing baseball. Although I learned a lot at school, sex education was not taught. Unfortunately, I learned about sex the wrong way in my father's shop. I learned about it in a life-damaging way. At that time, I went to school with both English and Amish children since the Amish did not have their own separate schools like they do today.

Even though we went to church every other Sunday as all Amish do, I never experienced anything real or alive. Those who spoke at our church services spoke in German, and I did not learn any German words until I was at least in the fifth grade. So, for me, church was a place that I just sat and behaved. God was rarely discussed in our home, nor did we pray. At one time my father did pray with our whole family. It was one Sunday night when I did not go to youth group. It was my mother, however, who actually made my father pray. He prayed a prayer out of a prayer book. I often wonder if my father, in forcing me to memorize Psalm 23, turned me off to the teaching of my church.

I remember a prayer that my mother taught us to say before we went to bed. It went like this: "I'm really tired, and I'm going to sleep now. I shut my eyes and I ask my Father and the angels to be around my bedside."

Although we prayed this prayer each night, having a personal relationship with Jesus was not talked about or encouraged in our home. The Amish church does encourage families to read the Bible each day, but our family never did that. So, during my childhood years I did not learn much about God even though we went to church. I had, however, developed a dark sense of who He was.

When I completed school in the eighth grade, I was 14 years old. As I said earlier, that cycle of sickness little by little stopped during this time. I continued to work in my father's shop, but now I was a full-time worker. However, I was not paid money because living in my parents' home was considered my pay. I worked Monday through Friday from 7:00 a.m. to 5:00 p.m. and Saturday until noon. Yes, the sexual abuse continued during those years in my father's shop.

As I approached the age of 16, I had the option of participating in *Rumspringa*, but I had no desire to participate. I wanted to stay in what I thought was a safer environment.

With that decision, came my parents' decision for me to join church. In the Amish culture, that is a very important and serious step to take. I soon realized that if I joined church, my father's beatings would stop since joining church was a step from childhood into adulthood.

As an adult, my father could no longer beat me. In fact, I did threaten my father one day after a beating. I told him that I would tell the minister about the beatings if they continued after my church membership. If our minister found out, my father would have had to confess his actions in front of the church. Those words were more than a threat, and my father recognized that.

I knew, however, that receiving freedom from my father's beatings was the wrong reason to join church. So, I did have some mixed feelings. Why, if I did not really desire to have a relationship with God, should I go through with it?

Since my parents continued to encourage me to do it, I went through with it out of obedience to them, but mainly so that the beatings would stop.

The spring before I turned 16, I went to the nine instruction classes required for membership. After those nine weeks were over, I, along with the others in my class, confessed Jesus as my Lord and Savior and I confessed that I would stay with the church. However, I really had no idea what it meant to confess Jesus as Lord and Savior of my life. In fact, I never knew God in any personal way, nor did I sense Him working in my life.

But, hallelujah, the beatings stopped. Actually, they had stopped after I threatened my father. I no longer had to nervously anticipate when the next beating would occur. Unfortunately, the sexual abuse continued in the shop and I kept it all a secret.

On a snowy and wintry day in March when I was 16 years old, my mother was admitted to the hospital. She was treated for severe depression. The electric shock treatments and medication helped but they certainly did not heal her. I did not understand why my mother was having so many problems. As she came home, I had high hopes that she would take care of the home, but that did not happen. She continued to be depressed, and I had to run the home. This made me angry.

The sexual abuse continued until one particular morning. While working in my father's shop, my abuser grabbed me and made sexual advances in a way that he never had before. At first I felt no fear because I thought he was just doing something different. So in my innocence, I once again said nothing. And he said nothing. But, what he did next shocked and scared me as never before, but at the same time my body was experiencing pleasure as never before. The confusion of mixed-up emotions was beyond what I could begin to comprehend. He took advantage of me that day in completely robbing me of the little innocence I had left. In reality, he raped me. Yes, he raped me right in my father's shop.

I told no one.

Only as this book has been written have I been able to call his actions rape. It was because of the pleasure of the sexual act giving such deep guilt and shame into my soul, that I personally felt responsible. But now I can call his actions rape, because he was an adult and I was only 16. At that time I was too uneducated about sex to understand what really happened. But he knew exactly what he was doing. (In fact, by the law's definition, what he did is called statutory rape.)

Although I clearly remember the events of that rape, I totally blocked out the memory of the rest of that day. Even now I cannot remember what happened the rest of that day. Maybe as I continue on this journey of healing, God will bring the events into my memory.

I do, however, clearly remember the events of the very next day as if it was yesterday. While I was sanding the carriages, this same man who robbed me of my innocence, started making fun of me and sang in a mocking way, "Naomi's pregnant, Naomi's pregnant."

I was immediately **horrified**. Although I was 16 years old, I felt like a tiny little girl during those very seconds. I felt as if a sword called betrayal cut my heart into pieces. Although I could see customers right outside the shop window, extreme loneliness gripped me.

Deep shame and tremendous humiliation quickly lowered my head and eyes. I actually felt like Humpty Dumpty who after falling off the wall, broke into pieces. I even believed that like Humpty Dumpty, "all the king's horses and all the king's men, couldn't put Naomi back together again."

My emotions absolutely overwhelmed me, and I wondered, "How could he ever sing and make fun of me after all he took from me, after all I gave to him?" I hated him, never wanting to be in his presence again.

This was a memory that I could not forget and I could not push it away. In my child-like thinking, I assumed he was right, because as a married man with children, I thought he must have been able to tell that I was pregnant. Just thinking about the possibility of being pregnant kept me mentally and emotionally troubled. Forgetting did not help me this time because I could not forget.

That night, waves of fear, shame and guilt billowed over me as I tried to sleep. I cried and cried and cried.

In my desperation, I cried out to God, questioning, "This can't be happening to me, can it?" I felt trapped. However, I could not let anyone in our house hear me cry for fear that they would ask what was wrong. That was especially hard because my sisters and I shared a bedroom. I did my best to hold back the tears until I knew they were asleep. I tried to plan what I would say if any one of them asked why I was crying. I just could **not** let anyone know!

I feared facing my abuser the next day. I guess he feared facing me too, because he gave me the cold shoulder. I was glad, so very glad. Yet, as each day came and went, I kept wondering if I truly was pregnant.

The nights in my bed were very long. I had no one to talk to. I had no one to ask questions. I was so afraid. I did not know what I was going to do if I was pregnant. But hallelujah, a couple of weeks later, I found out that I was not pregnant. Needless to say, I never had one more sexual contact of any kind with this man after that incident. I did my best to stay away from him, and he stayed away from me. Nevertheless, it was extremely awkward.

I wish I could at least say that there was no other man who took advantage of me in a sexual way. However, I seemed to be a magnet for boys and men to abuse. Between the ages of 16, shortly before I was raped, and 19, I was molested seven times. Each time, I either did what was asked, or else I did nothing while the men fondled me. Unfortunately, I said nothing and did nothing, because I was afraid. I do not recall which molestations happened before or after I joined church.

During all those years, the topic of sex was a big secret and never talked about by anyone around me except the man in my father's shop. It was even a big secret when a woman was pregnant like my mother. That is just how it was in the Amish culture.

Although more will be shared later concerning how the events of my childhood affected me, I do need to state how confused I became over the years. Deep down I knew that all those actions were wrong even though no one told me. I knew that those men were taking advantage of me, but I thought that I had no choice. I was afraid to tell anyone, not only for fear of getting in trouble, but because I never heard anyone talk about their sexuality. I had never heard of any other girl experiencing what I did, so naturally I figured something was wrong with me. I tried unsuccessfully to get rid of the feelings and memories so that I would not feel so guilty.

Let me explain more about my confusion. My abuser and his wife and children lived near us. This man not only worked for my father, but he and his wife were good friends of my parents. They would visit our family at times, and my sisters and I would walk over to their house and visit with them. I look back and wonder how I ever spent time with his family while he was abusing me. However, once I was raped, I never visited his home again.

Deep confusion resulted as I felt dirtier than the dirtiest trashcan, even though I liked the attention and the feelings that I received when I was touched. You see, touch and attention was something I had never received from my parents, so I liked it even though it was wrong. During those developmental years, I would secretly welcome those touches, and there was even an incident where I invited a man to touch me. This later caused me extremely deep shame and guilt.

In the midst of all this on-going confusion, I kept working in my father's shop, diligently avoiding my abuser.

So here I was—Naomi Lapp. I was a church member, an adult by Amish definition, a hard-working member of the community, and a supposed Christian. To the Amish community, I appeared normal and healthy. I carried on with life just like everyone else around me. But in reality, I was just a little girl with piles and piles of jagged-edged pebbles hurting my insides. I had no idea that they were there. I had no true concept of God let alone a relationship with God. In fact, I did not even have a clue who He was.

In Summary

The Amish place great value on families working together, and this easily happens because work on the farm requires the help of all family members. Families eat all meals together. And if the family is not a farming family, it is important to spend time together and work together however they can. If communication is good between family members, this type of environment can develop tremendous security in a child.

However, as you heard my story, you learned that our family did not hold to the normal values of the Amish. Our family did not work together. My father's carriage business did not require that. It would have been more of a blessing if our family had spent time together even though it was not required with my father's work. But since my parents did not value spending time together, we did not do that.

I only remember one time that our family ever did something together—the day we went to the zoo.

I never spent much time with my mother since I always worked in my father's shop. He and I never bonded together to have a healthy father/ daughter relationship. In fact, I received little attention from anyone except the men who abused me. I was never told I was loved. I was never hugged. And when I did need to work in the house, I had to "run the home" while mother was sick, putting a lot of stress on me. I developed a pattern of getting sick and doctors would find nothing wrong with me. My home life and relationships did not help me experience security.

In looking back, I now see that it was in my father's shop where I developed a lot of beliefs about myself. I felt very good about myself when I would stand back and see a magnificent carriage that I had helped to construct. Yet it also became a place where those painful events of physical and sexual abuse took place causing me deep shame, guilt, anger, fear, confusion, and insecurity. Every one of those events, whether good or bad, significantly molded me as a person. In summary, my father's coach shop was a place of both wonderful and horrid memories. It was a place that birthed many lies in my thinking about God, myself, and other people. It was those lies that produced my painful and extreme emotions.

It felt like I had a double life. Although I was involved in normal childhood play and activities, my childhood innocence was also being defiled at the same time. That was wrong, so very wrong. My life appeared to be okay, but it was not. I was a very confused and insecure child.

What did I do with the memories of those wrong childhood events that happened to me? Was I aware of the lies that I started to believe? What did I do with the painful emotion I felt from those lies? How did I handle the memories of being hurt and neglected? How did I process them? What did I really feel about what had happened?

The truth was that I did not want to think or feel because I did not understand. It was too confusing, and that confusion was immensely painful. It did not fit into my world because I never heard anyone ever talk about the things that I had experienced. So I found a way to not think or feel about the situations I could not understand.

As a child, all on my own, I discovered a way that I thought I could remove the memories with their painful lies. I learned as each confusing event ended, to suppress the thoughts and feelings of what had just happened, and cling to the hope and belief that the memories and feelings would eventually leave. I would then go on with my day.

Amazingly, I did that day in and day out for years, with no one telling me how to do that. During the day or as I went to sleep, when a painful memory would surface, I would just push it away. I would push it away very quickly. In doing that, I did not consciously think or feel anything about them. I was able to remain numb to what I really felt, and it became an automatic reaction. It became normal. This was the only way that I could cope and continue to work in my father's shop, even after I was raped. It made life easier and lighter, and at that time I thought I would be okay.

Although I did a great job of ignoring my memories and feelings, I had no idea that I was developing a belief system that was very ungodly. When I talk about a belief system I am talking about what I think about God, myself, and other people. My belief system, although hidden and not understood by me, was so wrong, so full of lies, so full of pain, and so very destructive.

I lived among a culture and church that did not address abuse in anyway, nor did it encourage the sharing or dealing with feelings. Counseling was rarely permitted. In essence, my culture and church helped to keep me numb and unhealthy. I am so grateful that some Amish are now seeing the need for counseling instead of denying memories with their painful emotions.

But as I said earlier, my memories of abuse, as much as I pushed them away, did not leave. They remained deep within, shattering my tender soul. Each painful memory, like a pebble, had its own jagged edges. Those jagged edges caused a lot of pain, grief, and poison; a pain that I worked very hard to not feel. It grew into a deadly poison. As the painful and poisonous pebble pile grew higher and higher and heavier and heavier, a mountain was forming. In the midst of this growing mountain, God was nowhere to be found.

All the confusing and painful memories with their lies and negative emotions were present, but I suppressed them. Those powerful emotions did not drive me to do things in my young adult years that many people often do in those situations. For instance as an adult and in my shame, I did not hide from people and become unsociable. In my guilt, I did not show a destructive behavior. In my anger, I did not walk in rebellion. In my fear, I did not run away from the responsibilities of life. In my confusion, I did not lose my mind. In my insecurity, I did not stop helping to make beautiful carriages.

Outwardly, I seemed okay and even happy. In fact, my behavior was acceptable, just like other Amish people. I did all the right things, but inwardly the lies with their painful feelings were working in a huge powerful demonstration; in fact, they were so much alive that they tried to speak to me. Instead of listening, I just kept pushing them away. I did not want to listen or deal with them. Consequently, little by little they spoke negatively to my spirit, soul, and body, and caused me all kinds of physical and emotional problems.

As I entered adulthood, my body was in an adult body that experienced adult sensations, but in reality, I was just a fearful little girl whose mind was full of lies about God, herself, and other people. With those lies, I had made vows that gave my life a wrong direction.

By the time I was 34 years old, all those lies with their deadly emotions began to surface through emotional and physical problems.

My Adult Years

After I joined church, I became involved in the youth group but never enjoyed it. I did not feel like I belonged with the other girls. They were always talking about housework and I just wanted to have fun. At times the boys played baseball. The girls would just watch and cheer. I did enjoy watching and cheering, although I would have rather played. The different youth groups in our area would often meet together and play volleyball or other games. It was at these youth group meetings that I met fellows. I dated some during those years, but I did not really like any of them. I felt like I was wasting my time.

For weeks, months, and years after joining church, I seldom heard anything about Jesus in my home or from my grandparents. In fact, I never gave God any thought other than when I was in church. God was distant. I did not know much about Him. But I did try to follow the rules of the ministers and bishops.

Once in awhile when I was not working in my father's shop, I would babysit children from other families. Although my father acted like he did not want me doing this, I was glad that he allowed me to keep the money. I saved $30 in my piggy bank from the time I was a child. This money came from babysitting and tourists who gave me money to allow them to take my picture. I used this money to buy my own sewing machine since every Amish woman has to own a sewing machine. Sewing was one of the few homemaker activities I really enjoyed.

One evening when I was at a volleyball gathering of different youth groups, I was curious about this one guy who was hanging around with my sisters' boyfriends. I found out that his name was

David Stoltzfus. We met later that evening. He was very kind and I just loved his curly hair and smile.

The next youth group gathering was held at my home, and I noticed that David kept looking at me and he kept hanging around me. After the last person left, David and I walked to my father's shop where he asked me for a date. I was so excited and believed at that moment that I was going to marry David.

The next weekend, David and I went to dinner with my two sisters and their boyfriends. We had a lot of fun together and hung around in my father's shop office after dinner. Before David left to go home, he asked if he could see me again the next weekend. Of course I said, "yes." That was the beginning of my life with David. At that time, I had no idea how God was going to use David in my life.

David was the son of a dairy farmer, and as his parents grew older, he took over their 60-acre farm. In my relationship with David, dating took on a different meaning. It was the month of April when we met. Life seemed to bloom with hope and dreams like I had never experienced before.

When I was with David, the thoughts of my abusers never entered my conscious mind; I only thought about David. Since I had done such a good job of suppressing those memories, I thought they were all gone.

David and I spent time together every weekend. We continued to date with my two sisters and their boyfriends. Eating dinner together was often our date. We also visited other friends and played volleyball.

One night in late August, we were sitting on the sofa in my father's shop office. We talked about many things including some mutual friends who were engaged. David asked if I thought they would really get married. I said "yes." He then asked if I thought we should get married, and I immediately said "yes." Even though the Amish wedding season was only three months away, we planned to get married at that time. Needless to say, I had a lot of work to do to prepare.

Although I was so excited that evening about marrying David, I did not wake up my parents to tell them. However, my sisters and I stayed awake as we excitedly talked about my wedding.

The next morning my mother asked if David and I had ever talked about getting married. I guess she was wondering if she should start preparing for a wedding that November. My mother was extremely on edge about the possibility of having to handle all the preparations in three months. When I told her that we were planning to get married, she immediately reacted negatively. Because she was ill at that time, she said she did not know how she would get all the work accomplished in just three months. She grew more ill, physically, mentally, and emotionally.

A cousin of mine was getting married the week after me, so David and I decided to hold our wedding at her house since it was easier to prepare one house, rather than two houses. As soon as I told my mother of our plans, she snapped out of her illness and was fine. Mother and I continued to plan our wedding together. It was difficult though because I felt like our wedding was a burden for her.

I imagine my mother told my father that I was engaged. He never said anything to me about my engagement. I also never told my abuser, even though I continued to work with him everyday. I did everything that I could to avoid him.

I never confessed my sexual abuse to our minister or my family as we were supposed to do at that time. Although I rarely focused on what happened with my abuser at that point in my life, I was inwardly very confused on how to handle this rule of the church. Not only was I continually pushing those memories away, now I was denying my responsibility to confess. I never had any intention to disobey that rule of the church, but it just seemed easier and lighter to avoid thinking about it. It was too painful.

When I think back to that time today, I clearly recognize that fear and shame kept me from telling anyone. I did not want to feel more fear and shame. Confessing would only have plunged me deeper into the fear and shame I worked so hard to hide.

So David and I were married on Thanksgiving Day in 1962. Love was all I could sense and feel that day. It seemed to be in every stroke of the crisp fall breeze that brushed against my rosy cheeks. David was 25 years old and I was 20. My dress was peacock in color with the white apron overlaying it. My sisters were my bridesmaids and wore the same colors.

We spent our wedding night at my cousin's home. The next morning we helped everyone else clean after the wedding. As most Old Order Amish did at that time, we stayed at my parents' home the next couple days. It was the custom that David would return home to his parents' farm on Tuesday and I remain home with my parents. David came on weekends, and we would stay in my parents' guest bedroom. This arrangement continued until spring when David's parents moved into the new house they had begun building when we had announced our engagement. Then the farmhouse was empty for me to move in.

Another common Amish custom included young married couples visiting families on weekends right after their marriage to receive their wedding presents. As we went from family to family and had wonderful visits with all of our friends, we received many nice gifts. We were also fed delicious meals.

In January 1963, a couple of weeks after our wedding, we went to Ocean City, New Jersey, for our honeymoon. We stayed with English friends who my father knew from his business and who lived near the beach. Although it was extremely cold, we walked the beach and the boardwalk for what seemed to be endless hours. We only stayed from Saturday to Monday since David had to return to his farm chores.

In April, David's parents moved to their new home and I moved in with David on the dairy farm. It was then that I stopped working in my father's shop. What a relief it was to be away from my abuser! I did, however, see him on rare occasions when I visited my parents. It was harder to see him those times because it stirred up painful emotions that were buried when I was not in his presence. In fact, during those rare times that I did see him, I could never make eye contact with him.

I now began life as a farmer's wife. Without seeing my abuser everyday, it felt like a new start for me. I loved to drive the baler which baled the hay, but I did not like to milk the cows. I did not like the smell of the cows. However, I eventually did work more with cows. I loved working with David and helping him. I even learned how to deliver a calf. And, by the way, I did create good meals for David in spite of my mother's concerns. In fact, David loved my cooking more than his own mother's cooking.

One day I told David that there was a man in my father's shop who "messed around with me." David asked me no questions and I offered no further information. I also told David about the beatings, but I did not tell him how bad they were. David, in his ornery way, said that I must have deserved them. I felt hurt, but as usual, I just suppressed those feelings.

My mother and sisters frequently visited David and I during the first year of our marriage. They helped me adjust to all the farm responsibilities since I had not grown up on a farm. They also helped me with housework. We had a lot of fun together. My sisters would also visit with their boyfriends. Those were good times together.

We were very happy the first several years of our marriage. Our farm was so beautiful with the sparkling Pequea Creek running right through our property. We would take frequent walks. I loved sitting on the porch. After growing up in town where there were a lot of people, I loved the quietness and peacefulness of our farm.

On March 2, 1964, our first son, John Lee, was born—almost one and one-half years after we were married. In spite of the difficult delivery, we were so happy to have our first baby. My daily routine drastically changed, but I loved it. Then five and one-half years later on October 11, 1969, our second son, Nathaniel David, was born. His delivery was easier than John's delivery. John was excited to have a baby brother and he learned how to help care for him. He even learned how to change his diaper. On August 11, 1973, Matthew Ben was born. His delivery was very easy. Each delivery became easier.

We enjoyed many wonderful family times together as we visited Ocean City, New Jersey, and friends in New York, and Indiana. We would pray together as a family in the morning and evening and at each meal. However, those spiritual times together had no significance until we visited friends in Indiana. Their prayers were personal and real. It affected me greatly because I realized that we had a dead spiritual life. I envied and wanted that real and deeper relationship with God that they exampled to us. Our little son, John, even noticed it, and asked, "Mom, could we pray like them in the morning and evening?" So we started to pray differently. And we also started reading the Bible together as a family. There were times I sensed God's presence, but it never lasted. It would merely come and go.

Life was wonderful then. I enjoyed it. I liked being around people and was well-liked by people. We hosted swimming parties in the creek on our property. Believe it or not, after my tomboy years, I felt fulfilled in my role as a homemaker, except in the case of mending clothing. I loved being a mother and spending time with my children. I hugged them and told them I loved them.

I made a vow as a child to not be like my parents. It was wonderful to have a home where there was love and communication and everyone worked together on the farm. There were times when I thought our children were too young to do certain tasks, but David helped me to see how important it was for them to be involved in helping.

During those childbearing years, my abuser continued to work at my father's shop, but I chose to visit only on Saturday afternoons because he only worked until noon.

My father rarely visited our home. If we needed something built, he would send workers from his shop instead of coming himself. I am so thankful that my father did not send my abuser.

My mother's visits would usually be strained. Tension would increase between us as she tried to control my home. She would even move our furniture. When she left, I would put things back. I understand that she would often visit because she and Dad were fighting, and the fighting depressed her. Later, she was placed on a medication that could be regulated, and her depression lifted.

During those years, David and I started a puppy business so that we could have additional income with a growing family. Our children just loved the puppies.

In the fall of 1974 when I was 32 years old, for some reason not known or understood by me, I became depressed and had no energy. A couple of months later, I started to experience a quivering within my body, especially inside my head. Picture in your mind the machine that shakes a can of paint so that colors can be mixed. Feel the motion of the paint can moving back and forth. That motion is what I felt inside my head. It was a strange and tiresome sensation. I had no idea what was causing it. Many nights I went without sleep, causing a deeper depression and less energy.

In June 1975 I became pregnant again. This pregnancy was not like the others. It was extremely difficult, and I had absolutely no energy. It seemed that my pregnancy would never end. Finally, Minerva Grace, our first daughter, was born on March 16, 1976. David and I were so happy to have a baby girl. Unlike my other deliveries, this delivery was horrendous, but I did sense God's peace and presence with me during that delivery. Unfortunately, however, the sense of His presence did not stay. I wondered many times after that happened, why it never stayed.

I could have no more children after delivering Minerva, but I was content and it did not matter that I could have no more children.

After Minerva was born, my energy level decreased. I could not even properly care for Minerva or the other children, both physically and emotionally. David's mother who lived next door, often came to help manage our home. A doctor suggested that I try some homeopathic remedies. It did help me to sleep and function better, although the doctor was confused about the quivering inside my head and was not able to relieve it.

In the beginning of December that year, my father had a heart attack and was in the hospital. David and I visited him one evening. I could not believe how friendly he was. Even though this encounter was so different, I still did not know my father. He came home from the hospital shortly before Christmas Day.

Then on Sunday, March 13, 1977, three days before Minerva turned one year old, while my father was at church, he dropped to the floor after shaking hands with some men. An ambulance was called. The medics tried to resuscitate him in the ambulance and at the hospital, but he passed away of a massive heart attack.

We knew that many people would be coming to the viewing and funeral so my mother did not want to have it in her home. Since a neighbor offered to have the services at their larger home, we accepted the offer. Hundreds of people came to his funeral because he was so well-known and liked.

Although we did not know our father well, we were devastated when he died. My mother did not know how to go on living because she did not know what to do about the carriage business. Unfortunately, my father never wrote a will. Shortly after his death, we discovered that the business finances were not what we thought. My mother was in great financial trouble. To help my mother, however, one of my father's former employees assisted her in extraordinary ways until my brother took over the business in 1978.

The shock of my father's death changed my life forever. The anger that I felt surprised me. I was extremely angry because my father had never apologized for beating me, nor did he ever appreciate the hard work I put into his business. Unfortunately, I was never in tune with how I felt about my father until he died. I could feel nothing but anger, and it was deep! I was so angry that I could not follow in my brothers' footsteps and kiss my father goodbye before his casket was closed. I did nothing about my anger after my father's death.

My health and emotional state started to become much worse at that time. For months I was miserable, and many days I just laid in bed. I did not go to church. Because the quivering, which was primarily in my head, caused an equilibrium imbalance, there were days that I could hardly walk. I continued to be depressed with very little energy. I visited many doctors, but no one knew what was wrong with me. I begged God to help me, but it seemed He never heard me. There were times I believed that my furious anger towards my father was the reason for my health problems, but in keeping with my normal coping skills, I continued to suppress my feelings.

The next spring in 1978, I was extremely depressed. As summer approached, all I did was cry. I could not be a mother. I could not be a wife. And I could not do housework. David would put the children to bed and say their prayers with them. I was not functional. I hated it when David's mother would help because I wanted to be the one to take care of my family. I was extremely discouraged and felt so guilty. We finally hired a neighbor girl to help.

Our children attended Vacation Bible School at a church several miles from our home. They would come home so excited about what they did and what they had learned. Their excitement in telling me the Bible stories was like a flame of fire to me. As a result, we even bought a set of Bible storybooks for the children to read. David and I read and enjoyed them as well.

One day in the middle of June, David's cousin, who lived three hours away in Brush Valley, came to visit. She and I had been talking regularly by telephone about all my problems. That day she packed Minerva's and my clothes and took us to her home. She thought perhaps that my getting away would be beneficial, and she wanted to help me with the natural products that she sold. She took care of Minerva, tended to me, and took care of her own family and home.

Everyday she would read excerpts from the *Guideposts* to me. The poems and stories greatly encouraged me.

While I was away, God again felt so close. I had peace. We returned home after ten weeks, arriving home the end of August. However, I felt worse, both physically and emotionally, than when I had left. And God seemed nowhere to be found. I wondered why.

David's cousin suggested that I visit David Mast, a nutritionist in Coatesville, as he could suggest some vitamins and supplements to make me stronger. I followed his suggestions, but I still had problems. Then, Mr. Mast suggested I see a dentist/nutritionist in Chicago whom he thought would help.

I called this dentist/nutritionist and in January 1979 I visited him in Chicago. I was diagnosed with hypoglycemia, TMJ, and collapsed blood vessels. At first the doctor had no idea why my head quivered the way it did, but he asked me if anyone had ever beat me. I shared about my childhood beatings. It was interesting that no other doctor ever asked me that question, and I had never once thought to offer that information either. The doctor thought that the beatings on my buttocks had damaged my sacrum which caused a misflow of spinal fluid throughout my spine and head. This was the reason for the collapsed blood vessels, the TMJ, and the quivering in my head. As I laid on my back, he moved my head in various positions and performed cranial treatments on my head. This would unlock the nerve energy to cause the proper flow of the spinal fluid.

While I was in Chicago, I visited the doctor's office each day from 9:00 a.m. to 4:00 p.m. He would work on my head for about one hour, and then I would walk for an hour. Then he would work on my head for another hour. This cycle of treatment went back and forth each hour from 9:00 a.m. to 4:00 p.m. each day.

I was ecstatic because I finally found a doctor that not only understood my problem but had a solution. The treatments helped me tremendously. I came home after one week. Hope not only welled up within my soul, but I had moments when it seemed to be spilling out of every pore in my body. How I wanted that hope to lead to my healing.

Mr. Mast and the doctor continued to consult together. Unfortunately, the doctor believed that I would eventually be in a wheelchair and die an early death. Mr. Mast was extremely sad at this diagnosis and visited me every single evening for about two months to give me reflexology treatments. One evening he told me about the doctor's opinion that I would die young. When I heard his words, I was confused. The doctor was smart, but yet it just did not seem possible that a wheelchair and death would soon be at my doorstep.

For about four years, I went to Chicago two times a year. These treatments cured my hypoglycemia and collapsed blood vessels, but I still had the problems in my head when my TMJ would act up. During those four years, my health and emotional state was up and down. Then little by little the treatments did not hold as long. So I went to Chicago five or six times a year for the next 15 years. However, I received no long-term healing from the quivering in my head. Little by little over those 15 years, I was getting worse. My symptoms continued to be depression, no energy, and quivering in my head. Lifting something or accidentally hitting my head, which I seemed to do often, would cause the flow of the spinal fluid in my head to be restricted.

I remember how lonely I felt going to Chicago. Yet in my hotel room, God often seemed to be so close to me. As usual though, that sense of God's presence which I longed to experience every moment, would leave when I returned home. I still did not under- stand what was happening.

During those 15 years of getting worse, we could not be a normal family because we could not do much together. Our family was certainly not an example of the Amish way of life. Yet, we were functioning just like my family. I was like my mother and grandmother. Because of my health issues, I did not appreciate people visiting, and we could not visit other families. We did, however, enjoy picnics along the Pequea Creek on our farm.

I could not attend funerals or weddings, and I hardly ever went to church. If I did, I would only stay for one hour. David and I would go home and leave the children at church. I would suffer greatly when I came home and then not be able to sleep at all due to the quivering in my head. For years, we could not host church on our farm.

Life also grew more miserable inside the walls of our home. David and our children had to run the home and take care of me. It was horrible. I wanted to die, yet I was not sure where I would go if I died. Sometimes I could not even sit at the table to eat because of the quivering in my head. John stayed home from school some days to help me. Or some days our hired girl did my cleaning, laundry, and cook- ing. Sitting out on our porch was a great help be- cause I could enjoy God's beautiful and peaceful creation. I longed for those moments, even though they were few and far between, when it seemed as if the splendor of God visited my weary and depressed soul.

In the fall when the silos had to be filled, I had to cook for all the men who helped. That was difficult and draining for me.

Fighting with David really escalated during those years and our children were upset by it. Our communication was poor. I would clam up and hold grudges just like my father. David would explode, but then forget what we fought about. Because I was the oldest in our family and David was the youngest in his family, I tended to be the leader and this caused more problems. As David would say, "I don't know," in situations, I would take over control. I was just like my mother. Although David felt that he was often angry and impatient with me, overall, I think David was most patient and kind to me during those years.

While my father was alive, he had built an apartment above his shop for guests to stay in while they were visiting. About a year after my father's death, my mother moved into that apartment, and my brother and his wife moved into the house in which we grew up. My brother and his wife had taken over the ownership and operation of the coach business.

On Labor Day weekend of 1983, a friend was visiting my mother. About 11:00 p.m. on Sunday, my mother heard an explosion and shortly after smelled smoke. She realized there was a fire downstairs in the shop, and yelled across the driveway to my brother. The only way she and her friend could get out of the building was to escape through the outside stairwell. By that time, the flames and smoke were worse and billowed over the whole structure. My mother and her friend did get out of the building. However, just about everything burned to the ground. We were grateful that the basic structure was still good and strong.

We were also grateful that our mother and her friend escaped. That very day her life seemed more precious to me. We were certainly relieved that only the shop burned to the ground and not the house as well.

I did question God though because I felt He was unfair to my mother and brother. We had lost my father and now we lost his business. My brother walked around in a daze. Within two weeks, however, our Amish friends totally rebuilt the shop and the apartment upstairs.

Although officials believed that the fire was started by arson, they never discovered the culprit. The business records from the time that my father started his business were lost. All of our pictures, including the pictures of the carriage we restored for the Miss America pageant, were lost. Because my mother lived in the upstairs apartment, she lost everything she owned. She cried and cried, especially when her friends would visit. The house next to the coach shop had an available downstairs apartment, so mother was able to move in right beside the coach shop and right beside my brother and his family.

In the spring of 1987, we built a log cabin home on the property of our farm. Our son, John, got married and he and his wife, Kati, moved into the log home for four years. About two years later, our son, Nathaniel, married Linda.

In March 1992, John and Kati moved out of our log cabin home to a home in Dauphin County. So David, Matthew, Minerva, and I moved into our beautiful log cabin home. We were so happy to live in our dream house. It was as if life gave us a big gift in the midst of years of medical bills that never seemed to end. It was much smaller so I did not have as much area to clean which made it easier for me. We rented our farm to friends, and they farmed the 60 acres for five years.

When Matthew and Anna Ruth got married, they moved onto the farm, and took over the dairy farm with David's help.

In the spring of 1997, David and I were visiting some friends. While there, we received the news that David's cousin, with whom Minerva and I had stayed when she was one year old, had committed suicide. Needless to say, we were shocked, absolutely shocked, because she was so kind, outgoing, and giving. She seemed so strong as she took care of me, Minerva, and her family. We kept asking ourselves, "What caused this?" We never received any answers. We only felt deep hurt.

During all those years, I continued to have the same health problems as I went from doctor to doctor, trying to find someone to help me so I would not need to travel to Chicago. But I found no one. So five to six times a year, I traveled to Chicago.

After all those years, 23 to be exact, from the time of my initial depression in 1974 until Christmas of 1997, I still was depressed. I was numb. I had no energy. I felt confused. I still had the quivering in my head. I still felt hopeless. I often held a death wish close to my heart. And now I began to think that the doctor in Chicago was right; I would be in a wheelchair and die soon. That was what my life was like.

I could not understand why no one could help me, and I often wondered why God's wonderful presence seemed to come and go. I would ask, "Where are, you, God?" Although I knew God existed, He was certainly not around me. He was cold and distant and, at times, seemed dead.

The Beginning of My Healing Journey

Our children were upset about David and I fighting so much, plus they were concerned that I was not getting better. So they did something that Amish people rarely did at that time. For our Christmas present in 1997, they sent David and I to counseling.

We did not tell our minister right away because counseling was looked down upon within the Amish culture. About six months later, however, David did tell our minister and we were very encouraged to receive his support for me to receive counseling. Our children made it clear that they wanted me to receive counseling first. Initially, I did not want to go; however, as the date drew nearer, I really wanted to help our marriage especially in the area of communication. I went to Life Ministries in Conestoga and was assigned to a counselor named Elaine. My first session was January 13, 1998, and our son, Nathaniel, went with me.

When I arrived, I was asked to complete a questionnaire, and I stated that I wanted counseling so I could have a better relationship with my husband. Little did I know what God had in store for me through counseling.

When I entered Elaine's counseling room, I immediately felt at ease. Her room was so bright and cheery as the radiant green colors, which seemed to saturate the atmosphere, awakened my lifeless spirit. Her personality and smile calmed my anxious spirit and made me feel most comfortable and welcomed.

When I sat down, I immediately started to talk. Elaine did not need to even get me started. In that first session I talked about the disagreements that David and I had concerning where our coffee table should be located in our home. The location of that coffee table in our living room was very important to David and me, and it became a big issue. I also shared my feelings about David's cousin who had committed suicide. I was still upset and wondered how and why that could have happened.

As I talked, I could not believe that Elaine was not only sitting right in front of me expectantly waiting to hear my innermost feelings, but she cared enough to really listen. At the age of 55, this was certainly a new experience for me. It felt good.

What I also appreciated about this counseling session was that while I was sitting on the chair in Elaine's office I could look out the window and see a picturesque pond. The scenery captured my heart and caused my thoughts to naturally turn to God. I just loved sharing my feelings, and could not wait to return for a second session.

During this time, my mother and I were spending good quality time together. We were getting to know one another, and I loved it. Unfortunately, she had developed heart problems and the doctors gave her a pacemaker. It helped her tremendously, but then she also developed Parkinson's disease.

About two weeks after I had my first counseling session, snow and ice blanketed our area. As I looked out our back window on that cold Monday morning, the glistening of the snow and ice seemed to suddenly wake me up. Every window in my home looked like a framed picture of the purest and brightest winter wonderland. It was absolutely breathtaking. But I was sad because I did not feel well. The quivering in my body, especially in my head, once again started up. I became more depressed and angry as I thought about my physical condition. I did not want to make another weary trip to Chicago, and I found myself not caring about anything. I decided to take a walk down to our dog kennel located about 700 feet behind our home. Walks would usually help me release some of my anger and give me new energy.

Unfortunately, in my disgusted and discouraged "I don't care" state, I walked out our back door without boots on my feet. I knew I should have put on boots, but I did not feel like going to the basement to get them. I walked very carefully down our back steps and towards our dog kennel. I could hear and see the form of my feet crunching through the ice and snow.

Little by little the ice was getting thicker and thicker with no give for my feet. All of a sudden, as I was walking on the downgrade, approaching the entrance to the dog kennel, I felt the momentum of gravity pulling me. I sensed that I was in really big trouble and tried to stop, but before I knew it, my buttocks hit the ice. A split second later my head hit the ice. I laid there while sparkling stars seemed to dance before me in the backdrop of the beautiful blue sky. After lying on my back for about five minutes, I slowly got up and walked into the warm kennel. David had no idea where I took my walk, so I just sat there until I gained my composure. I warmed up and then began what seemed to be the longest walk of my life, as I walked back up the hill. I think I walked slower than a snail, but I made it home safely.

Feeling nauseated, I laid down most of the day. David wanted me to go to the doctors but I did not want to go. However, I finally gave in and called the doctor in Chicago later that day. He suggested I take a homeopathic remedy. It helped temporarily, but I could tell that there was more damage in both my back and head. Three weeks from the day I fell I traveled once again to Chicago for more treatments.

I was only going to stay one week, but I had to stay ten days because of the fall. I came home feeling much better, but I had to rest.

Since I did feel better, I rescheduled my second counseling appointment. However, I was not able to get one until May. In that second session, I talked about a situation with David and our son and daughter-in-law's Bob White bird. Because David did not take my advice, their Bob White bird died in David's hands. That upset me so we discussed it. I also talked about my physical problems. As usual, it was difficult to explain what my body was feeling since my symptoms were unusual. I thought Elaine might understand since she was a nurse, but like all the doctors I saw, she too had a hard time understanding what I was feeling physically.

I returned for a third and fourth session and talked about our marriage and other issues a bit more important than the coffee table and our Bob White bird. I tried to seriously listen and asked questions so I could understand Elaine. Because I grew up in an environment where feelings were not felt, shared, or processed, I did find it difficult to keep up with Elaine. I often went home feeling miserable because I could not figure out what was going on inside of me. I had to think about what I was feeling for a day or two and then call her on the telephone and we would discuss it. After I thought about our session for a few days and after we talked on the telephone, I really understood what Elaine was saying to me.

About my fifth session, David also came for counseling and he met with Dan. David did not want to go at first, but the more he counseled the more value he saw in it. He met with Dan for about a year. Some sessions we met together, but most sessions were separate. When we were together, we often discussed my medication issues. I had seen a psychiatrist who put me on Lithium. He worked with

Elaine. They thought Lithium would be helpful since it had helped my mother, but it made me worse.

At the beginning of each session, Elaine would ask me what I wanted to talk about. I appreciated that. Surpisingly in my fifth session, the secrets of my sexual abuse just came rolling off my tongue. I had not even planned to talk about it. However, the words just came out faster than I could control my tongue. I could not believe that someone finally knew.

During all the months of counseling, I only remembered one of the seven other times I was molested. I finally shared that memory too. During those months I also talked about the beatings that my father had given me. I felt deeply ashamed in exposing my father's actions, yet it felt so refreshing to get it all out. It took many, many sessions to share all the facts and my feelings. Interestingly, I found myself praying to God in those sessions like I had never prayed before. It felt so good. It gave me a calmness that I had not had for quite awhile, and I loved the sense of His presence during those times.

That summer in 1998, I felt relatively good—physically, mentally, and emotionally. I was relieved to tell Elaine my secrets. Nevertheless, I knew that something within me was still not right. As the fall of 1998 arrived, all my symptoms came back in full force. I was tremendously depressed and my body was once again not functional.

Because we were tired of paying the costs of traveling to Chicago, I called an osteopathic doctor in our area and told him about my physical problems. He said he thought he could help, so I scheduled an appointment. His one treatment, however, not only made the pain in my head stronger, but it also caused pain in other parts of my head. The nerve pain from my sacrum to the right side of my head was excruciating. A pulling developed that went from underneath my jaw, over my heart, and down to my sacrum.

Moving down my left arm and left leg, it felt as if threads were ripping apart every two to three inches. In reality, nerves were actually splitting. As they split, they would form lumps on my left arm. I could not sleep on my right side, lest I wake up screaming in pain. In addition to that pain, I now felt as if concrete blocks were on my shoulders. It was a constant severe pain. I stopped counseling that fall into the winter because I did not have the physical strength to travel the 40 minutes to and from Elaine's office.

To understand the sensation I experienced in my body, tie a rubber band around one of your index fingers as tight as possible. Keep it on until the tip of your finger turns red and the area begins to pulsate. Notice how your finger feels real tight as if it would explode. That same tightness and explosive-like feeling is what I experienced inside the right side of my head and down my left arm and left leg. However, the tightness would build to the point that I did experience explosions. In reality, like I stated above, those explosions were my nerves splitting. This condition stumped the doctors.

So on Thanksgiving afternoon of 1998, I was back on the train to Chicago. For the first time in 19 years, however, the treatments did not help. I felt like it was a wasted trip. Discouragement as to how I felt was an understatement. While I was receiving treatments during that week, I grew worse and reached the point where I could hardly walk. The constant pain on the right side of my head always seemed to find its way down my left arm and left leg. I wondered, "Who would help me now?" I not only wanted to die, but I really thought I was going to die. I began to think that the doctor was right. I would die soon.

Since I could hardly walk, David had to come to Chicago to help me return home. He arrived during the night, totally exhausted, but when he got to my hotel room, in his exhausted state, he patiently talked with me about what we would do if I died that night. What would David do with my dead body? I did not want to be buried in Chicago. What if I never saw my children again?

However, the doctor assured David and I before we started for home that I would not die. So, with my excrutiating pain, we started our 18-hour train trip home. I could not sit, stand, or lay longer than a couple of minutes. It was a most horrendous trip, not only because of my pain but because I had no hope of anyone helping me. Death was all I wanted.

But, hope came knocking at my door. When we finally arrived home, I told David that at least I could still pray. That was an amazing statement in light of the fact that I had no personal relationship with God. Knowing that I could pray brought me hope.

David kept insisting that I go to the hospital. I did not want to go because I was so tired of the treatments that never helped, but I finally gave in. David called an ambulance, and I went to the emergency room. Of course, the numerous tests showed nothing. Those doctors, like other doctors, asked if I was in my right mind and sent me home with pain pills.

It was not easy to sit at home and think about those trips to Chicago. I often thought about how I would stop and sit by a certain waterfall as I took my required daily walks. As I sat and enjoyed watching the waterfall from my blanket, God seemed so close to me as I sensed His presence and love for me. How I grew to love that waterfall over the years. Those visits were like a kiss of heaven to me, but, unfortunately, all those loving feelings would leave me when I returned home. Life felt so disappointing and sad. I was very depressed.

As January of 1999 arrived, one of our puppy customers suggested that I visit Jefferson Hospital in Philadelphia. In desperation, I made an appointment. The doctors discovered that the fifth and sixth discs in my neck were herniated from my fall on the ice. They advised that an orthopedic surgeon examine me. So off I went to be checked by an orthopedic surgeon. But, he wanted me to see a neurologist first. So off I went to be checked by a neurologist.

The neurologist only gave me a 50% chance of success with surgery and demanded $45,000 up front for the surgery. But, the neurologist did schedule an MRI to check the blood vessels in my head. Of course, there were no new discoveries. In fact, I was told that my blood vessels looked like that of a 16 year old. So back to Jefferson I went with my MRI results, only to be told that they could not help the pain in my head.

But, I was sent to an ear, nose, and throat specialist. Neither did he find anything wrong. You can imagine how I was extremely weary of doctors and appointments and tests. And I wondered where God was in all of those hard times, and questioned His ways in my life.

In the spring of 1999, I went back to counseling because of my depression. Elaine suggested I get anointed with oil by Lester Miller, the founder and director of Life Ministries. I agreed. On May 11, 1999, Lester, Elaine, Dan, David, and I met together. As we all sat around a big table, I felt like I was going to collapse. Lester put oil on my forehead and prayed for my healing, both physically and emotionally.

From the moment that Lester put oil on my forehead, I felt a heaviness, an uneasiness, confusion, guilt, and a lingering darkness. It was horrible and worse than ever. I did not know why, but I was too afraid to do or say anything.

During the anointing, I kept focusing on the fact that I did not feel right within myself. After the anointing, Lester told me that he felt so weak that he almost had to sit down. I still said nothing because I was afraid to find out why I felt the way I did. I went home feeling discouraged and more depressed because even an anointing could not help me.

During the night, I decided that in spite of my fear, I needed to tell Lester what I felt during the anointing. The next morning I called Life Ministries and much to my surprise, Lester answered the telephone. I told him what I had experienced and we discussed the strangeness of the anointing, but arrived at no conclusion.

About the time I was anointed, my family doctor sent me to another orthopedic surgeon who gave a 75% chance of success on neck surgery. Since I was miserable, I thought "why not," so, off I went to prepare for surgery. On June 1, 1999, my neck was operated on. Because of all my physical problems, a bone was taken from a bone bank instead of another place in my body.

Can you guess the results? Even though my neck healed wonderfully, I still had the same pain on the right side of my head. I returned home to a hospital bed in my living room, thinking that I would lay in it for a couple weeks. However, I laid in that hospital bed for one whole year.

Pain was the theme of each day. Day after day, week after week, month after month, it was so depressing to look out my front window and watch all the people passing my home. On Tuesdays and Wednesdays I would see the Amish women walking by as those were the days Amish women would meet and do things together. How I longed to be with them. I was growing angrier and angrier.

The only desire I had during that year was to die. I would ask David to pray that I would die, and I would tell him to marry another woman. One day when our son, Matthew, came up from the farm to visit, I remember telling him, "Please take care of father."

Matthew cried.

Deep down inside though I knew that I wanted to live. I was truly fighting the greatest battle of my life because I had no hope of ever getting better. I could hardly walk because I had no balance. I had to crawl to the bathroom and refrigerator. I could not sleep. David had to bathe me. I had to hold onto the sides of the bathtub while he washed my back because the washing motion caused spinning and tightness on the right side of my head. David had to feed me. I would scream during the night. The nerves inside the right side of my head and my left arm and left leg continued to split.

Over the years I had grown to absolutely hate the nighttime darkness. Why? Because night hours were extremely long due to my pain and sleeplessness. When the morning sun peered through our bedroom window, I felt exhausted and dreaded another day. It was a vicious cycle. I dreaded the days. I dreaded the nights.

Many times, David and I felt hopeless about our finances. We were constantly spending any money we had, and I was only getting worse. Looking back, I could relate so well with the lady Mark taught about in Mark 5:25-34 who had been bleeding for 12 years. It says in verse 26, "and had endured much at the hands of many physicians, and had spent all that she had and was not helped at all, but rather had grown worse." Like her, I went to many doctors, spent all our money, and was getting worse.

David would sit and wonder what was wrong with his wife. I felt so badly for him because I could not be a normal wife to him. Through those years I often watched him do all the chores around the house. He would take care of the children, and then he would have to take care of all the cows, both milking and feeding. Over and over as I watched David, I realized that I was seeing an example of Jesus. Yes, he was not always perfect, but he was often patient, compassionate, and loving towards me. And then there were times he would push me to try harder when I was in pain and had no energy. When I did what he pushed me to do I was okay. David was truly a gift of God's mercy and grace. Many mornings I would tell David, as he left to tend to the puppies, that I would be dead upon his return. But, I was always alive when he came home. There were days he believed me, but over the years, he grew numb to my comments.

In August, I decided to visit Elaine again for counseling. I could hardly endure the ride to and from her office, but I persevered. We talked many times about the deep confusion that I felt and experienced in my sexual abuse. I cannot tell you how "used" I felt by men. As far as the man in my father's shop is concerned, I came to understand that I was just his "side pleasure." I knew that what this man had done to me was wrong, but as time went on, in talking with Elaine, I finally came to confess out loud that what he did felt good to my body. I admitted that I found myself welcoming his touches as I walked into my father's shop. That was extremely difficult to admit in counseling, but when I did, I found more peace.

During one of those sessions, my deep and dark, hidden secret came out. I finally told Elaine that one day I had intentionally made a comment to encourage him to touch me. Releasing that secret brought the greatest relief I had ever experienced in my entire life. I had instantaneous peace. There was no longer any fight inside of me. At this point, I realized why Lester and I felt the way we did during my anointing. Unknown to me, I harbored a deep dark secret that held back God's power during the anointing. Elaine and I continued talking about my feelings concerning my abuse.

At the end of each session, I felt I had told it all. But there was still more. I would come to the next session and yet another memory would come into my mind. I can honestly say that little by little, as I released my secrets to Elaine, God became more real to me. I seemed to see His work in nature like never before. I sensed His presence with me in more consistent and greater ways. That presence brought a beacon of light to my entire being. It was life-giving. I felt more secure with God and myself. Here I was, a 56-year-old lady finally letting out the secrets, and admitting my responses and reactions. It took me a long time to understand.

Six months after telling Elaine my deep, dark secrets, she suggested I be anointed again. Although I agreed with her initially, I did not want to follow through with that since the first anointing was of no help. The day and night before the scheduled anointing, I was very sick. I hardly slept. I asked David in the morning why I should be anointed again since it did not help the first time and since I was only going to die anyway. David ignored my comments and insisted I go. David and I went. I had to go into the back entrance of Life Ministries because I could not go through the front entrance and up the steps. Just the thought of walking up those steps drained me.

Upon our arrival, we sat around a big table. David, Lester, Dan, Elaine, and I were present. In their presence, David and I had about an hour session of confession. David shared things from his heart and I shared things from my heart. After a time of confession, we sang a song entitled, "Thank You, Jesus." We sang it over and over.

Lester then put oil on my forehead. Everyone was standing around me. As he began to pray for my emotional and physical healing, the heaviness lifted from me. In a short period of time, I felt as light as a feather. I felt clean. I felt pure. I felt forgiven. Everyone began crying.

Lester told me later that the Spirit of God was so strong as he reached to put oil on my head that he could hardly touch me. I could not believe the difference from the first anointing. I had no more questions or doubts or confusion. God had showed Himself to me in a very powerful way. It was truly a delight to my soul.

I left Life Ministries that day feeling extremely refreshed. I felt forgiveness, purity, and peace as I walked confidently down the very steps I could not walk up. Out the door I went. I did not schedule anymore sessions with Elaine, but I did talk with her on the telephone.

After the anointing, I enjoyed a peace I had never experienced in my life. The early morning hours were full of hope for a good day. The evening hours had no dread of sleepless nights. The sunsets behind our home appeared more breathtaking. Life was peaceful. Although I still had the pain on the right side of my head, my depression was not as deep.

One day I went to a Christian bookstore where I wanted to purchase my own Bible so I could learn more about this God who was healing me. I also pur-chased a small poster. The poster intrigued me because I felt very in touch with it. It was a picture of a big mountain with pebbles at the base. The word-ing, *God Moves Mountains, One Pebble at a Time* fascinated me. That picture seemed to be a descrip-tion of what was happening in my life.

A couple of weeks after my anointing, Elaine suggested that I read the book entitled, *The Healing Path* by Dr. Dan Allender. Although I felt forgiven, pure, and peaceful on the inside, my body was still so weak and full of pain.

Each evening David would read a couple of pages to me as that was all I could handle. As David would read the book, my thoughts kept turning to my abuse. One night, I could bear it no longer. I asked

David to put the book down. It took me about 15 minutes, but I finally told him the truth about my sexual abuse, and I told him how bad the beatings were from my father. David did not say much. He just listened. I will never forget how I could actually breathe better once I told David everything. It was like weights were lifted off of my chest and shoulders. I sighed and sighed and sighed. David asked me why I waited so long to tell him. I told him I did not know how to tell him.

Every night David kept reading little portions of *The Healing Path* book to me. I was greatly encouraged to be able to hear something that helped me so much. In that book I learned about another girl who was beat by her father and sexually abused by another man. In fact, that little girl's mother, like my mother, knew about the beatings but never stopped them. For the first time in my life, I realized that what happened to me happened to someone else. I no longer felt alone. Never in my life had I been exposed to the truth that Dr. Allender taught in that book.

Little by little, I began to see how God protected me throughout my life. He protected me from getting pregnant when I was 16 years of age. He protected me from dying. He protected me from taking my own life. He protected me from losing my mind. He protected my marriage. He protected my children and now He was giving David and me grandchildren. And I could see how God, at different times, allowed me to taste of His presence and beauty in the midst of my pain.

The fall before I was anointed the second time, our church minister and his wife told me of a doctor at Johns Hopkins University Hospital in Baltimore, Maryland, whom they thought may be able to help the pain in my head. He was a psychiatrist and his name was Dr. Andy Warren. I contacted him and much to my surprise, Dr. Warren came to my home shortly before Christmas in December 1999. I was still in my hospital bed.

The evening he came to our home there was a wagonload of Christmas carolers singing outside of our door. It was so nice because he was able to enjoy their melodious songs.

Dr. Warren was so warm, asking me to call him Dr. Andy. He talked to me for some time and left some medication for depression. I took it for one week, but it did not help. In fact, it made my head feel tighter. Dr. Andy suggested I go to Johns Hopkins University Hospital so I could be monitored. I had to wait for a bed date, and it finally came through to go on April 5.

Although plans were made to go, I kept asking God for a sign as to whether I really should go to Baltimore since I was tremendously weary of doctors and tests. One day a friend from church stopped by and told me she knew there was still something that was going to help me, and she believed I should go to Johns Hopkins University Hospital. She had known nothing of my plans to go.

Even though I appreciated this affirmation, the night before I traveled to Baltimore I sensed death was at my door. I definitely knew that if I died that night, it would be more peaceful than other times I thought I would die because the anointing had taken the edge off my depression. So the next morning I was off to Baltimore.

When I arrived, the doctors and nurses performed many tests attempting to discover what was wrong. They discovered that I had "affective disorder." I was put on two medications. One was Paxil for depression from a chemical imbalance, and the other was Zepraxa for the nerve pain. I had to go to classes for grief, emotional healing, managing pain, and how to relax before going to bed.

The first two weeks I got worse before I got better. Until my medicine was adjusted correctly, it was hard to walk in the hallways. Many days I had to use the wall for support as I walked down the hall. I also had to attend exercise classes. After about two weeks, however, I found myself suddenly getting better and better. I felt ecstatic and very hopeful.

I did attend church and really enjoyed it. In fact, some days nurses, who were on break, came with me. There was a statue of Jesus in the hospital chapel. I used to go up to it and touch Jesus' hands where the nails had been. As I got better, I started to think that God really did care about me

I met so very many nice people during my stay. Many people were in pain like me. Although their pain differed, it was pain. As I grew better, I found myself ministering to and encouraging a lot of these people. They said that they saw a huge change in me from the time I had arrived. They, and even my doctor, asked me many questions about God and my faith. I just loved those interactions as I could share what I saw God doing for me and in me.

Finally the day came when I could go home. It was May 12. I did not walk out of the hospital that day. After laying in a hospital bed for one year, I excitedly hopped, skipped, and jumped out of the hospital as a new woman!

It was better than the hopping, skipping, and jumping my sisters and I did through the puddles as young girls. I *knew* that God was with me. Life was now bright instead of dark. My faith was growing stronger and stronger as my spirit, soul, and body were getting healed. It was great! And I wanted to know more and more about God and who He was and how He worked.

As I arrived home from the hospital on May 12, 2000, after a five-week stay, I truly felt like a new woman. I felt no depression and my head had no pain. I only had a slight tightness on the right side of my head. As soon as I arrived home, I walked down to Matthew's farm. It felt so good to walk and breathe the beautiful spring air. That walk seemed to be the most beautiful walk of my entire life.

I was not home real long before I wanted to do volunteer work to help people. Through Elaine's suggestion, I applied for a volunteer position at a hospital in Lancaster. In June I began to work there on Fridays, pushing patients around the hospital, and carrying blood from the patients to the labs. I loved it. I mean I loved it after all those years of being sick and alone. I also applied to work at a nearby farmer's market. I obtained a job and worked there every Wednesday. It was wonderful to be around people.

My life became different—very different. On Wednesdays and Fridays I could stand all day and work. Wow, what a difference! I went to church. I visited people. People visited us. I helped with yard work. I could walk to the refrigerator instead of crawling. I could walk to the bathroom. David no longer had to bathe me. I could cook. I could clean. It was like a dream come true. I finally had my life back together.

The fall weather was absolutely invigorating.

The holidays were full of peace and joy and love.

I rejoiced!

The year 2000 was a wonderful year.

.

God's Redemptive Plan

In January 2001, David and I took a trip to Pinecraft, Florida, for the very first time. How wonderful it was to travel for fun instead of traveling for my health! We had a wonderful two-week vacation visiting Amish friends and relatives. I felt normal. I felt real. Most of all, I felt true to myself because my secrets were exposed!

While we were in Florida, I told one of my friends that I would like to share with her what God had done for me. We planned to talk that next day. But, lo and behold, when I arrived at her home the next day, 25 Amish and Mennonite women were sitting in her living room, eagerly waiting to hear my story.

I started sharing about my childhood days all the way through to that very day. I spoke from my heart. David sat next to me as I talked. He was a great help in sharing the big picture of my life.

Surprising to me, those ladies appreciated hearing my story and how God worked in me and through my situation. They all shed at least a tear or two and shared big hugs to each other and me. Many of the women had known of my sickness, and they rejoiced to actually see me there in Florida. It was a miracle to them. I also could tell that they really appreciated my honesty in sharing, which is rarely found within the Amish and Mennonite community.

David's cousin, who also lived in Pinecraft, heard my story that day. She invited me to come to her home and share with another group of women. So a couple days later, David and I went to her home and about 18 women were there. Their reaction was the same.

Here I was in the state of Florida for the first time, and it was the first time and place I publicly shared my story. For me, Florida really did become that "sunshine state," which it is often called by people.

I returned home feeling so very full of sunshine myself—so encouraged to not only see how hungry the Amish and Mennonite women were to hear my story, but to see their need to be in relationships where life's pain and struggles are talked about in an open and honest way. It was actually overwhelming.

I also left Florida deeply encouraged to see God using me. In fact, He was actually using what happened to me to help others. In spite of the years I complained and fought with God, I could not believe that He still valued and loved me enough to take me to Florida. I was humbled, truly humbled. On the trip home, I had flickering and hopeful thoughts that God would use me again.

During the time that we were away, my mother's Parkinson's disease grew worse. When we returned home, I spent a lot of time taking care of her and enjoyed this time. She loved to sit in her front window and watch all the people browsing and shopping at a tourist attraction across the road. For months, I remember her just sitting and calling for my sister-in-law, but when she would visit, my mother would have nothing to say.

Taking care of my mother caused me to think about my life in a way I had never thought about before. During those days, I came to realize how much my relationship with God had changed. It was now a personal relationship, no longer distant and cold. I could see the value of exposing secrets in counseling, because the exposure of those secrets caused my soul and spirit to become free. In becoming free, I could hear from God. God's presence was continually becoming more real and consistent.

I reflected upon the fact that although I had heard about God's gift of salvation, I was never able to embrace it until my secrets were told. I also came to realize that if I had died or committed suicide at any one of those times I desired death, I would have gone to hell. Plus, I came to realize that God was really working in me during those few times I did sense His presence. He was working to bring me to salvation, and He was working to heal me so I could help others. It was as if I could see a golden thread in my life. And that golden thread was Jesus.

Life was taking on a different picture. It was becoming like a beautiful bouquet of flowers with radiant colors and inviting smells. In fact, I could finally see the radiant colors and smell the inviting fragrances. Oh I wanted so intensely for those flowers to continue to bloom and blossom.

During those days of taking care of my mother, I also thought about the Old Order Amish church. Although salvation is taught, involvement in Bible studies and prayer groups is not encouraged. I have come to believe that those kinds of gatherings were very important not only for my spiritual growth, but for my emotional and mental health. I also came to realize that I wished there was more encouragement to understand and learn about the work and ministry of the Holy Spirit. As God was revealing those truths to me, a hope and desire to help women was growing.

I amazingly discovered during those days and months that I did not have to keep pushing the memories away. It was okay to think about them. If I wanted to think about them, I could. If I did not want to think about them, I did not have to think about them.

I now had a choice. I **really** had a choice, and I actually had peace when memories entered my mind. What a difference! As the pebbles, one by one, lost their jagged edges, the pile shifted and the mountain was moving. With the mountain moving, the person of God was becoming clearer and clearer.

One late afternoon in July of that year,   as I was walking down the road in front of our home, a car passed, stopped, and backed up towards me. The lady driving the car rolled down the window and asked if I knew who she was. I told her she looked familiar, but I did not know her name or from where I knew her. She told me that she was Sharon Hershey and that we had gone to school together as children. She also told me that she prayed for me every time she drove past my house since she had heard I was so sick. I started sharing how God was healing me, but cars were passing making it difficult to converse. So, I asked her if she wanted to come to my home so I could tell her more of my story. Since Sharon's husband was not coming home for supper that evening, she came and visited. We spent several hours together and had a wonderful time of sharing.

I found out that evening that Sharon had started a ministry for women called Wellspring Garden Ministries. Sometimes I would pass this place and wonder what it was about. What an encouragement to hear that it was a ministry to help women. Sharon and I decided to keep in touch with each another.

When Sharon left, I knew deep down that I would somehow be involved in Wellspring Garden Ministries. I was especially excited because Wellspring was near our home. I could even walk to it.

As I sensed a plan unfolding, I began to think about the word *redemption*. I had often heard it in church, but I did not really understand what it meant. However, for the first time I was beginning to understand it as I saw how God was going to use my abuse for good—His good. He was actually going to redeem the wrong that was done to me. Even though so much time had passed and I was getting older, He would still redeem my abuse and use me. Romans 8:28 says,

"And we know that God causes all things to work together for good to those who love God, to those who are called according to His purpose." This verse told me that God was going to cause everything that happened to me to work out for good.

I began to believe that God definitely had a special plan for me. He had a purpose. He even had a purpose for my abuse. What a revelation! Although God's plan was different than what I would have done, I could see that His way was the most effective way for me to help women. My experiences, which the devil meant to destroy me, would instead be the very experiences that God would use to help other women. I found this new understanding of redemption very exciting, yet extremely humbling.

On weekends, during that summer, my mother would stay with us. For the first time in my life, I was sharing with her from my heart. We were really getting to know each other. After much pondering, I decided I would not tell her about the sexual abuse I experienced nor the way the beatings she had instructed my father to give, had affected me. I did not think it would be wise, and to this day I am glad I did not burden her with those heartaches. We just had good times together.

In late August my mother's health grew increasingly worse, and her hospice nurse told us that her days were numbered. One evening in particular when I was putting her to bed, I gave her a hug and told her that I loved her. Her sheepish response of "Oh, my" while throwing her frail arms up in the air, was all she could give back. It was very obvious that she did not know how to respond. It seemed to embarrass her, but it was very fulfilling to extend my love to her. As I already shared, showing affection and the sharing of feelings was something our family did not do.

I desperately wanted to have peace in my heart towards my mother before her death. Now, I did.

On the morning of September 4, 2001, her hospice nurse said that she would soon pass away. So all of my siblings and their spouses immediately came to mother's home. As the morning progressed, we could see that her heart was growing weaker and weaker. We had the opportunity to say "goodnight" to her, and as we stood around her bed and at about 12:00 noon, she passed away. The peace I had was humbling. I knew she went to be with my Jesus. I knew I would see her some day.

Of course, her passing was nothing like the passing of my father. With my mother I had time to learn to know her. I had time to get my heart right. I had time to show her love. I felt satisfied and content. I had peace. Sadly, getting things right with my father was something I never had the opportunity to do.

God gave us beautiful weather for my mother's viewing and funeral. No words can explain how different I felt inside for this funeral in comparison to my father's funeral. I kissed my mother goodnight, and although I was sad, my heart felt good—real good.

That November I took a Biblical Counseling Course through Life Ministries. The classes went through March 2002. I worked hard reading the nine required books and loved all that I learned. It helped me to become stronger emotionally, mentally, physically, and certainly spiritually. I was excited because I received good grades. That encouraged me because I was 59 years old at the time, and I had not had any schooling since 14 years of age when I finished school. In fact, I was the oldest lady in the class. It was also rewarding to take this course at the very place where my healing journey began. Only God could do something like that.

During the months after meeting Sharon, we spoke at various times on the telephone. Sharon invited me to come to Thirst Quencher, a Wednesday morning women's group at Wellspring Garden Ministries. Thirst Quencher was a place where women could share their lives and feelings and be heard without experiencing any judgment or criticism. I went. As soon as I walked into the building, I felt at home, wanted, and loved. After that first gathering, Sharon asked me if I would share my story at Thirst Quencher. Of course I was excited to do that, and we planned for me to share in January.

In January 2002, between classes, David and I made a second trip to our Amish friends in Florida. We traveled with *The Royal Sounds*, a gospel singing group. We played a lot of games and sang many songs on the trip down and back. In Florida, I was able to see everyone from our first trip. It was a wonderful reunion. Once again I was blessed to travel for fun.

Shortly after we arrived home from Florida, I shared my story at Thirst Quencher. There were about 14 women in attendance. It was even more healing to share with these women, because I felt like I was where I belonged. I have been serving at Wellspring ever since that day.

I began sharing and listening to a lady who attended Thirst Quencher. I also answered the telephones for Sharon on days that I was needed. I also completed various workbooks that helped me on my healing journey. I not only understood myself better, but I also began to learn more about my incredible God.

In the spring of that year, I went with two of my friends to a church in Philadelphia to hear Dr. Dan Allender speak. He wrote *The Healing Path* book that David read to me while I was in such misery. We spent three days listening to Dr. Allender talk. It was so wonderful to actually hear the person whose insight and wisdom concerning sexual abuse helped me so much. Elaine also went and, together, we soaked up all his thoughtful insights.

Since we had visited Florida, I was receiving phone calls from ladies who wanted me to share my story. Word had even reached my hometown area, and they too asked to hear my story. So one Thursday morning, I invited 20 women to come to my home. As I shared, we all cried. Pain reflected itself on almost every face. I could feel and see the need for women to hear my story.

Shortly after that meeting, Life Ministries asked me to speak at a women's monthly fellowship group in a church about 20 minutes from my home. Of course I agreed and went that morning anticipating what God would do. About 70 women were in attendance. I again saw the same tearful reactions and left with the same overwhelming feeling of need to share.

Through inheritance money that David and I received from my mother's estate, we planned to take a trip to Europe for six weeks that coming May. We were so excited. It was like a dream coming true for me. I went from being confined in a hospital bed, unable to walk for one year, to traveling to and through Europe. I knew that it was only God who could ever make something like that possible.

During those months of improved health, I periodically went for body reflexology adjustments. One time the pain on the right side of my head grew worse again, and I was so afraid that my symptoms would return. Fear overwhelmed me because I wanted to go to Europe so bad! I called Dr. Andy and he suggested that I increase the Zepraxa I was taking for nerve damage. I followed his instructions and within a couple of days, felt fine again. What a relief!

We wanted to travel to Europe so we could learn about our Amish roots in Germany, but also visit a friend in Germany. We left on May 24 and arrived home on July 4. It took us six days by boat to arrive, and then we traveled 3,000 miles by bus for the next two weeks before spending ten days with our friend in Germany. It was the most wonderful trip of my life.

As is the custom among Amish, our church had given us money to pay the bills from my neck surgery and my stay at Johns Hopkins University Hospital. Because of their financial help, we were able to use the inheritance money from my mother's estate for that trip to Europe. To this day, David and I are deeply grateful for our generous church.

Over the years I frequently told God that if He healed me, I would write a book to help others. I talked with Elaine about it different times. She gave me the names and phone numbers of some people whom she thought might be interested in writing. The Holy Spirit, however, never prompted me to call anyone on Elaine's list.

During those months as I was ministering at Wellspring and meeting with women one on one, I discovered how many women were hurting so badly. Plus, it was such a tremendous joy for me personally to listen and share with those women. Through all my experiences, I learned that it is safe to talk. It is okay. Talking is needed for healing. If we do not talk, problems will grow worse. Satan uses the dark place of secrets to destroy God's children.

In January 2003, friends invited David and me to attend a training session on prayer ministry. We had no idea what this entailed, so in our curiosity we attended. It was a fascinating time in learning how the Holy Spirit can, though prayer, minister to childhood wounds and hurts. We were taught how to pray with someone so this can happen. For me, it was life-changing to learn that the Holy Spirit could actually be my counselor. In fact, I learned that day that the Bible teaches that the Holy Spirit should be our counselor. I never knew that before. We also had time to gather in small groups and practice on each other.

As we divided into groups, my friend who took us to this training actually went first and then an-

other man followed her. It was incredible. The Holy
Spirit took those two people back to childhood memories. They both cried. We watched their body language
speak the pain of the memory, and then we saw peace
as the Holy Spirit delivered them from their pain.
When it was my turn, we had to take a lunch break.
As I ate lunch, I felt a growing fear of what might
surface in my memories. I wondered if it would be an
embarrassing memory. Fortunately, God gave me
peace, and I continued eating.

After lunch we gathered again in our groups.
I really liked Diane, our leader, because she had such
a quiet and soft spirit. I closed my eyes. Diane prayed
and asked Jesus to take me to a painful memory.
Immediately, He took me to a specific time when I
was beat in my father's shop. The pain was so
tremendous as he over and over beat my buttocks. I
felt unloved, unwanted, lonely, sad, and extremely
fearful.

As I felt this tremendous physical and emotional pain, Diane asked me if I saw or sensed Jesus
anywhere. How could I? But all of a sudden Jesus
appeared and said, "She's my child, you have no reason to beat her."

Jesus then began to touch my black and blue
marks with oil. I asked Jesus why my father did this.
Although I did not hear a voice, I sensed Him saying,
"He is frustrated and lonely."

Yes, I overwhelming and immediately experienced understanding and peace. During those precious moments, the presence and ministry of Jesus
enveloped me in such a powerful way that I did not
even want to leave the memory. Instead of pain, the
memory now had peace, love, and an understanding
of my father attached to it.

I realized that I had also made a vow as a result of these beatings. The vow was, "If I ever have
children, I would never tell my partner about the

beatings so they will never get the idea to beat our children." That vow had stopped me from telling David the truth about my beatings.

During this painful memory, I also experienced the most phenomenal presence of God. It's impossible to put it in words. I felt so loved, so wanted, and so happy. I no longer felt loneliness or fear, but totally energized and alive!

After that session, I kept thinking of the life-changing value in allowing the Holy Spirit to be the true counselor. What a way to receive healing!

I knew that a deeper healing happened to me that day. It was a powerful ministry, for sure. I was also eager to learn more about prayer ministry as Jesus could bring His healing touch to so many other people.

I took Diane's telephone number that day so I could keep in contact with her. I thought she could mentor me to help other women through prayer ministry. She agreed. Diane and I went to breakfast periodically, and we learned to know each other.

In the spring of 2003, David and I went to Phila-delphia so I could again hear Dr. Dan Allender speak. Although this gathering was only for one day, I was again greatly encouraged. And guess what? Mr. Allender was standing all by himself getting a drink of water from a water fountain. I went over and shared how his book helped me. He thanked me for sharing and said, "This just made my day." I was grateful to God for giving me that opportunity to connect with him.

Shortly after hearing Mr. Allender for a second time, a girl named Linda came to babysit for our Thirst Quencher meetings. Sharon had worked with Linda at a Christian residential center for single mothers in Lancaster City. The ministry had closed and Linda was not sure where God was directing her, so in the meantime she started driving Amish to pay her bills. The day she came to Wellspring she had her four-year-old nephew, Airick, with her. Oh, I immediately liked Airick a lot. He was so full of energy and life. As I got to know Airick, I loved how he would say whatever was on his mind, and I envied that because, when I was a child, that level of honesty was discouraged.

Linda became my driver. One day shortly after we met and while she was driving to Life Ministries for a support group meeting, I shared my desire to write a book. Without hesitation, Linda immediately volunteered to write it even though she did not know where she would be working. I could not believe God brought someone right to me. I did not need to call anyone from the list that Elaine had given me.

Sharon had talked to Linda about ministering at Wellspring in the past, but she was not confident that was where the Lord wanted her. However, now that she had committed to writing my book, she started volunteering at Wellspring. The ministry where Linda had worked and lived in Lancaster sold their building, requiring Linda to move by Labor Day weekend. She moved in with David and me.

Linda started to write this book in August of 2003. In the fall I went to another training workshop on prayer ministry, and I learned more about this personal Holy Spirit who lived inside me. I was fascinated. While at this training session, I met a woman who wanted to experience prayer ministry. Shortly after the training, she telephoned me one morning and asked if I was available to take her through prayer ministry that day.

I told her I could help, assuming that Linda would be with me to help. However, I found out that Linda was not available that day. I immediately wanted to reschedule, but Linda had confidence in me that the Holy Spirit would use me. So, depending entirely on God in hopes that I would remember some of what I had learned, I met with this woman and led her in prayer ministry.

Wow, the Holy Spirit ministered to her in a powerful way and gave her some instantaneous healing that day. I was so happy, to not only see what the Holy Spirit did, but to also see how God used me who had been so broken! I was ecstatic and praising God. This continued to strengthen my faith.

As October and November progressed, my health again began to deteriorate. I grew more and more discouraged, and could not believe that God was letting this happen. How could God let me down like this? During this time, an apartment in the Wellspring building opened up for rent, and Linda moved in two months after moving in with us.

Because I was sick, Linda did not accomplish much in writing this book. By the time Thanksgiving arrived, she stopped writing. I was sick throughout the winter with my head experiencing so much pain. Once again I started to lose hope. One evening the Board of Directors and staff of Wellspring came to my home and I was anointed. It was a beautiful time of singing and praying. That anointing gave me a new hope that I would get well.

Linda and Sharon were both convinced that there were still some unresolved issues that were causing my illness, so Linda suggested that I meet with Diane regularly for prayer ministry. I scheduled a session with Diane in the spring of 2004, and that began a series of prayer ministry sessions.

It was in those sessions and at times when I lay sick in bed, that six other molestations surfaced in my conscious memory. Although I state those events in one sentence, the consequences of each one of those events was very destructive in my life.

However, as Jesus ministered to each event in different ways, He always brought His healing life and peace into my pain. For all those months I had thought all the darkness inside of me was gone. But I was wrong. I had been molested and never even remembered. Through all those years, I did not need to push those memories away because they never even came into my conscious memory.

How exhilarating it was to have the Holy Spirit, the Spirit of truth, take me to those hidden places of pain. He was my counselor just as the Bible teaches. It was amazing! I can now truly thank God that I became sick again. The reason was to return to counseling so the Holy Spirit could surface those hidden memories that continued to affect me.

In the beginning of April shortly after I began sessions with Diane, I went to Johns Hopkins University Hospital once again for five days. The doctors put me on new medicine and I was sent home. I was fine for two weeks, but after two weeks, the head pain started all over again. What do I do now? Again, I felt that overwhelming hopelessness.

Someone who knew about my illness, sent me information on a Christian health clinic in Utah that helps people struggling with unresolvable health issues. It is called the Young Life Research Clinic and it was started by Mr. Gary Young, a nutritionist. In May I went there by train.

I never experienced a place like this clinic. Dr. Roger Lewis, my doctor, and the other staff were such caring and loving Christians. They first worked to cleanse my body through juicing and colonics. I could not believe all the toxins that flowed out of my body. Then they worked at rebuilding my body by placing various essential oils on my body. Biblical passages were even taught to support the use of these oils. I came home after five weeks, and since that time I have been continuing to work on both keeping my body cleansed and rebuilding my body. I have never felt so great in my life. David puts oils on me often and they continue to heal me.

Oh, I still have issues which need addressed and I will be dealing with them until I reach heaven's doors, but I praise God that I have been weaned off all of my medicine except for my thyroid medicine.

I now know that in eternity past, God planned to create me with a purpose. He allowed my abuse and hurts because He had a plan to not only heal me but to use the story of my abuse in helping other people. That plan is unfolding day by day, month by month, year by year.

I share with many women and help them walk through prayer ministry. Jesus ministers in many ways and I have the blessing of watching Him heal. I observe instantaneous healing causing their everyday emotions and behavior to drastically change. It is very exciting, but yet humbling. There is absolutely nothing like watching the power of God in a counseling session.

I do have a great burden in that I wish my Amish friends would talk more about their emotions, talk about their pain and bring it to Jesus, the true source of healing. Linda tells you about Jesus in the chapter entitled "Pain and Its Source of Healing." Taking your pain to Jesus is the beginning of healing and freedom.

Hallelujah! Although, I am now age 62 as this book is printed, I will yet again hop, skip, and jump in joy for my God!

God is good!

My Healing Journey

You can see from my story that healing did not come in one instant. Sometimes God does that in people's lives and sometimes He does not. Although instant healing would have been wonderful, I would have missed out on the "beauty" of the journey.

It has been in the journey that I have learned about myself, my God, my family, and my friends. It was in those moments of learning that I was humbled. Yes, it took many years to receive this measure of healing, and I continue to receive healing from painful memories, but I can truly say that at the time of the writing of this book, I sense that I am deeply healed.

I thank the Lord because only He can receive the glory. Over the years of abuse, those jagged-edged pebbles were formed, and now they are being made round and smooth through the healing process. By that I mean that the memories are there but no pain is attached to them. I can think about them, but I no longer feel the shame, the guilt, or the anger. That is because the lies within the memories were removed. If there is no lie, there is no pain.

I know that the Lord healed me, yet He also worked through other people and situations. For instance, entering the counseling ministry, although it was not until I was age 55, was the greatest step towards my healing. At that age, I was certainly well past the time to face those shameful memories, lies with their painful emotions, and the hard issues that I kept pushing away my entire life. How I thank our children for that gift of counseling.

As I talked and talked and talked with Elaine in those sessions and shared my secrets, it brought me deep comfort. In fact, my body actually felt a tremendous relief as my story was told. It took me about one year to share everything I could remember. And at the end of each session when I thought I had no more to tell, a continual flow of yet more memories, feelings, and issues kept surfacing. Surprisingly, it was healing to just hear me put it all into words.

The first thing I learned in counseling was **how to process the events** that happened to me, because I did not know how to do that. I was "locked up," and had to learn **how to feel**. I was an expert at pushing away my feelings.

I also had to learn, once I allowed a feeling to surface, to **identify what feeling it was that I felt**. I had to learn how to **identify my thinking behind those feelings**. And I had to learn how to **identify the effects of specific situations or events** that happened to me. I had no idea how to make those connections. When I learned how to do that, it opened up more discussion between Elaine and I.

Experiencing an anointing the second time was another milestone in my healing. The Bible talks about this in James 5:13-16 where we are instructed to confess our sins, pray in faith, sing praises, and call the elders to pray to anoint us with oil in the name of Jesus. What I experienced in my second anointing was life-changing. I actually felt a poison leaving my body that day.

Telling all to David was another huge step towards my healing. In fact, David, himself, was a big part of my healing. He was a picture of Jesus having so much patience and giving so much encouragement within our home. It really did help me get through those dark and dismal days.

Exercising which was usually walking, eating healthy, and taking vitamin supplements was also necessary to my healing. I thank the Lord for all the available natural and healthy foods and supplements of not only our own farm, but also accesible within Lancaster County.

Traveling to Florida and Europe was good for my mental state after being confined for so many years.

When I was put on two medications, I really started to feel better, especially on the right side of my head where the nerve pain was so strong. Currently, I am only on one medication and that is for my thyroid. I marvel that I am doing so well. I know that addressing all the pain inside me had the most impact on my healing.

When I shared my life story in Florida, I began to put my life into perspective. As the women responded in a positive and eager way, I could see a glimpse of God's purpose to my abuse and sickness. That was a huge help to me and a necessary step towards seeing God redeem all that was wrong. Telling my story was healing.

When I experienced prayer ministry, I knew that I was really on my way to deeper healing because Jesus took me to those deep and hidden memories I did not remember on my own. Although I was fearful, those sessions with Diane were so life-giving. I found that I needed to continue the sessions as this book was being written because the writing of this book caused additional hidden memories to surface. It felt like it would never end. Although I never went through a deliverance session, I know that during those sessions, I experienced deliverance from the dark side of evil. As Jesus entered my pain, I could actually feel that dark side leaving.

Meeting with women, one on one, and leading groups at Wellspring Garden Ministries has caused me to experience the power of God using evil for good. As mentioned earlier, I have seen the truth of Romans 8:28 come alive because it teaches that God causes all things to work together for good. When I think of my life, I can truly say that God does work all things together for the good of those who love Him.

I never thought I would receive so much fulfillment in leading support groups. It reminds me of my childhood times with my sisters when we tearfully consoled one another in our pain.

In looking back over my years of counseling, I now understand the value of good relationships. Whether it was my counselor or a friend, it was their walking alongside me, their relationship, that helped me tremendously. Healing comes quicker if you have people to walk with you as you go on this journey.

Healing also comes quicker if you have a counselor who models a healthy relationship with you. Many of us who travel this journey of healing do not know how to experience healthy relationships. We need to be taught. Our counselors can help to teach us that.

*   *   *   *   *

On the next pages, I share some of the details concerning the issues I had to finally face. They are broken down to hopefully help you learn how childhood situations and events in one's life can affect one through their adulthood. The issues I had to face are numbered because it was those issues that I and other people could see that put me in counseling. Then I listed the specific situation or event together with how I was affected and the belief(s) that I developed. Some issues listed vows if they were made, and at times comments were made.

You will notice that I was primarily affected in "emotional" ways rather than carrying out incorrect and unhealthy behaviors. That is because within the Amish culture, you are to carry out right and correct behaviors regardless of how you feel. So I was careful to do all the right things while stuffing inside what I felt.

I was "in tune with" some of my beliefs and vows, although others I was not. However, they eventually were uncovered as I traveled through my healing journey. The important thing one needs to understand is that although most of the situations listed below happened in my childhood, most of the affects, beliefs, and vows did not surface until I was an adult.

Here is a simple illustration.

Situation: While screaming loudly, a mother often tells her little girl that she is stupid.

Effect: She *feels* stupid.

Belief: I *am* stupid.

Vow: I *will* be stupid.

Long-term consequence: As a result, this girl may never live up to her potential. Unless she makes a conscious choice to receive healing, her feeling, belief, and vow will determine her life choices. Hence, we have "**long-term consequences of childhood abuse**." Or to say it another way, "**everyday she will live out her childhood pain**."

I trust that this chapter will help you understand how situations and events affect us. The information can become technical and quite challenging, because many of the issues and their details overlap. In fact, sometimes the issue is the belief. But in the overlapping, you will better understand what I had to deal with in counseling. I hope it helps you to understand yourself as well.

It is important for you to realize that my responses and reactions to my hurts may not be the same for you. As you will learn in the last chapter of this book, each of us has different personality traits that cause us to deal with our hurts in differing ways. Hence, we may have different responses and reactions.

As you read, you will see the confusion in my life. I also hope that you come to understand how **everyday I was living out my childhood pain**.

ISSUES I HAD TO DEAL WITH IN COUNSELING

1. Depression.
- ***Situation/Event Causing Issue:*** Developed a pattern of denying and stuffing my memories and my feelings.
- ***Effect(s):*** Felt numb; unable to function in normal, everyday activities and responsibilities.
- ***Belief(s):*** If I just push memories and feelings away, I will be okay. I am just like my mother.
- ***Vow(s):*** I will not think about things that make me feel dirty and shameful.
- ***Comments:*** I have learned that since God created us with emotion, it is very important that our emotion is felt and expressed, not denied and stuffed away somewhere. God has emotion and He expresses it. Handling emotions like I did was extremely unhealthy, even deadly. I also learned that because I am human and live in a fallen world, I will experience painful events and do wrong things. However, God helps me get through those experiences.

2. Physical problems.
- ***Situation/Event Causing Issue:*** My physical and sexual abuse.
- ***Effect(s):*** Depression; sacrum problems with nerve damage; hypoglycemia; TMJ.
- ***Belief(s):*** I am sick because God is punishing me. I am sick because of all the rootbeer I drank as a child.
- ***Vow(s):*** I will never get better.
- ***Comments:*** Over the years, I have learned that my childhood events greatly affected my physical and emotional health because I had

continually stuffed the memories and feelings.

3. Reality of the sexual abuse.

- **Situation/Event Causing Issue:** Pushing away memories and feelings all those years kept me living outside of reality.
- **Effect(s):** Emotional and physical sickness.
- **Belief(s):** I do not have to face my abuse because I will be okay. No one can find out what happened because they will think badly of me. No one, especially my mother, would believe me if I told them. This is too embarrassing to talk about to anyone.
- **Vow(s):** I will never think about the memories I push away.
- **Comments:** This was my first hurdle. Facing what actually happened to me made me face the shame, guilt, fear, anger, and confusion that I had pushed away for so many years. Just hearing my voice talk about these events was healing. I finally came to realize that Jesus took care of those deadly feelings. I could lay them down, after I did my part.

4. Sexual abuse was my fault.

- **Situation/Event Causing Issue:** Because I did not stop it, I thought it was my fault.
- **Effect(s):** I became broken inside as a person; guilt; shame.
- **Belief(s):** I should have stopped it.
- **Comments:** Elaine kept telling me over and over again that the sexual abuse was not my fault. She made it clear that my abuser was an adult and he had no right to do what he did to me. I learned that he took advantage of my curiosity, my innocence, my body, and who I was as both a person and woman. He used me. By the time the Lord brought the six other molestation memories to my mind, I understood this truth much more and the effects of the event were resolved more quickly.

5. Molestations.

- **Situation/Event Causing Issue:** I was molested seven times in addition to what happened in my father's shop.

- *Effect(s):* Fear; confusion; shame; guilt; anger; frustration; trapped; sexual problems in beginning of marriage.
- **Belief(s):** I must be dirty. God does not care about me. Something must be different about me that this keeps happening to me. I guess I deserve this because it keeps happening.
- **Vow(s):** I will never trust a man.
- *Comments:* I came to understand that this was a spiritual realm issue. Sexual spirits came into our family at least through my father, if not others. Those sexual spirits set me up for this to keep happening to me. When I met David, I just knew I could trust him and through the years he has helped me tremendously with that trust issue.

6. Why didn't I run? I should have.

- *Situation/Event Causing Issue:* I could not run from my father's beatings because he held me down over his knees. But, as an adult, looking back at the situation, I could not understand why I did not run from the sexual abuse.
- *Effect(s):* Guilt.
- *Belief(s):* I must have been pretty stupid back then.
- *Vow(s):* I like this and will never stop it.
- *Comments:* Over a long period of time I came to realize and admit how I liked the feelings I received from the touch of my abuser, and that is why I did not run. I finally came to realize that God designed me in a way that to be human means I am sexual. It was okay that I liked the feelings. And I came to realize that I am a sinner living in a fallen world.

7. Why did I ever start this?

- *Situation/Event Causing Issue:* I asked questions about sex and then I got fondled.
- *Effect(s):* Shame; guilt.
- *Belief(s):* I started this, so why quit. I am already defiled, so why stop it. I can't stop it.
- *Vow(s):* I won't stop this.

8. Loss of my innocence.

- *Situation/Event Causing Issue:* All of the sexual activity my body experienced.

- **Effect(s):** Anger; guilt; shame; violation
- **Belief(s):** I am less of a woman. I do not know who I am as a woman. I am damaged.
- **Vow(s):** I will never be a loving woman.
- **Comments:** This is a tremendous loss to any woman.

9. Did I "deserve" such beatings?

- **Situation/Event Causing Issue:** The beatings were so painful that I would wonder what was wrong with me that caused them to be so bad.
- **Effect(s):** Unworthiness.
- **Belief(s):** Something is wrong with me. What is it? I am my father's target for his frustration.
- **Vow(s):** I will never beat my children.
- **Comments:** I came to understand that both my parents were wrong in allowing such horrendous beatings to occur because the beatings were more than unreasonable. I also came to believe that my parents had their own problems in beating us the way they did. It wasn't about me or anything wrong with me. Jesus also made it clear to me in that first prayer ministry session that my father beat me out of his own frustration and loneliness. Since I have received healing, I have often felt sorry for them.

10. My parents not telling me "why" I was getting beat.

- **Situation/Event Causing Issue:** Of all the beatings I received I only knew the reason two times. The other times I received beatings I could not think of anything I did wrong that day or even previous days for me to get beaten.
- **Effect(s):** Shame; anger; bitterness.
- **Belief(s):** My parents were cruel people.
- **Vow(s):** If I ever have children, I will always explain their wrong behavior to them.
- **Comments:** I never came to any conclusion on this issue. But I had to forgive my parents and accept the fact that they did not tell me why I was getting beaten and that the "why" probably isn't important to know.

11. Why was "beating" their form of punishment?

- **Situation/Event Causing Issue:** I often wondered about this because of the level of pain and bruises I experienced on my buttocks and hands.

- *Effect(s):* Shame; felt belittled in return for all the ways I helped my father in his shop; major physical problems.
- *Belief(s):* This is unfair. My parents are cruel people. They have no compassion.
- *Vow(s):* I will never beat my children.
- *Comments:* This was another area where I had to forgive my parents and accept the fact that they did this to me. But accepting was not approving it. There is a difference.

12. Father.

- *Situation/Event Causing Issue:* He was absent, moody, gave the silent treatment, showed no expression including compassion, showed no affection, and gave no attention.
- *Effect(s):* Felt unwanted; unloved; angry; confused; shame. Carried out father's example of giving the silent treatment when I was angry.
- *Belief(s):* My father is very mean. My father does not love me. My father is very selfish. I do not think my father loves my mother. I am not lovable or worth loving.
- *Vow(s):* I will never be like my father.
- *Comments:* Although I had to deal with the negative emotion that gripped me, forgiveness was truly the only way out of this one. In my adult years, I did turn out to be much like my father. I had emotional problems and I gave the silent treatment when I was angry.

13. Mother.

- *Situation/Event Causing Issue:* Since father was hardly home, my mother took control of the home, often in unreasonable ways. After a certain age, she could not function as a wife and mother because of depression.
- *Effect(s):* Anger; took control over our marriage and home when David and I got married.
- *Belief(s):* I must stay in control of my home. My mother is not able to be my mother. My mother

will always be sick. I'll never get my mother's attention. I will always miss out on life.

- **Vow(s):** I will never be a mother like her.
- **Comments:** I made a vow to never be like my mother, but just as vows go, I did. I became extremely depressed and controlling. Because David is the last born in his sibling order, he just allowed me to control. This has been a hurdle for David and me. We are still working on this because it is not God's design for marriage and family. I became non-functional, just like my mother; in fact, I became more non-functional than her.

14. Hatred for parents.

- **Situation/Event Causing Issue:** Not loving me and showing me love; beating me; work was always the priority over fun and relationships with them.
- **Effect(s):** Depression; physical sickness.
- **Belief(s):** All my parents ever think about and care about is work. My parents do not love me, especially my father.
- **Vow(s):** I will never be like my parents. I will hug my children. I will tell them that I love them.
- **Comments:** I grew to hate them as I grew up, but as I forgave them, the hatred had no hold over me. In fact, it left. Forgiveness was the only way out.

15. Telling David about my abuse.

- **Situation/Event Causing Issue:** I did not tell him the full truth before and after we were married.
- **Effect(s):** Dampened our intimacy.
- **Belief(s):** I cannot tell. If I tell him, he will think badly of me. If I tell him, he will think he has a worldly woman.
- **Comments:** Believe it or not, this was another big hurdle for me. I had only told David a little about what happened with the man in my father's shop and a little about the beatings. Although I never talked with Elaine about telling David, it weighed on me that I needed to tell

him. When I did, I felt better; I could breath better as if a concrete block fell off my shoulders.

16. Confusion.

- **Situation/Event Causing Issue:** Sexual abuse was wrong but the sexual feelings I experienced truly felt good to my body; parents did not get to know me, parent me, or love me; running the home as a mother, but being a child, when my mother was sick
- **Effect(s):** I did not value sex as God did; I did not like to be around my parents; I developed unhealthy control which caused destructive issues to surface within our home and marriage.
- **Belief(s):** I am messed up. There is no way out.
- **Vow(s):** I will always be messed up.
- **Comments:** Sexual abuse is wrong and makes one feel dirty, full of shame, and guilty. Yet, the act itself brings sexual pleasure and a desire for more because of what it is. Elaine taught me that it was okay that I liked the sexual feelings I felt. God made humans to be sexual, so I came to understand why I felt so confused.

17. Loneliness.

- **Situation/Event Causing Issue:** Not bonding with parents; receiving no attention from par- ents; as an adult, being sick for such long peri- ods of time wherein I could not be with people.
- **Effect(s):** Bonded with a man in my father's shop in a sexual way, receiving his attention; resentment in not being with people while sick.
- **Belief(s):** This is my punishment for messing up my life. I am alone. God is not helping, so why talk to Him anymore. I deserve to be alone.
- **Vow(s):** I will always be alone because I deserve that.
- **Comments:** The pleasure of the sexual abuse tried to fill my emptiness, but it only broadened the hole. So, I felt very lonely and this feeling became more intense as I got older. I experi- enced loneliness on a deep level because I truly

had no comfort within my being. Although David and my children were great overall, they could not comfort my soul. As my secrets came out, the loneliness lifted. My experience was that God's love filled the hole of loneliness. If it was not for God, I would still feel lonely, to this day.

18. Hopelessness.

- **Situation/Event Causing Issue:** Never getting better, especially when the doctor in Chicago could not help me any longer; always getting worse both physically and emotionally.
- **Effect(s):** Desire to die.
- **Belief(s):** There is no way for me to get better.
- **Vow(s):** I will never get better.
- **Comments:** I knew that it was not healthy to think and feel that way or to ask David to pray that I die, but I often found myself at that place of desiring to die. I could not help those over-whelming desires. But as God was leading me to the right places and people for help, including Himself, hope grew inside of me.

19. Death.

- **Situation/Event Causing Issue:** I wanted a way out of my pain.
- **Effect(s):** Hopelessness.
- **Belief(s):** Death is the only way out of my pain.
- **Vow(s):** Death is my answer.
- **Comments:** This was the darkest, most evil place to be. Some days I wanted to die. Some days I truly thought I was going to die yet I was afraid I would die. And I was not sure where I would go if I died. I always had a fight, however, in me to live.

20. Anxiety.

- **Situation/Event Causing Issue:** Waiting to be beaten; knowing that the sexual abuse was wrong and keeping it a secret; the man in my father's shop mocking me about being pregnant; wondering if I was pregnant.
- **Effect(s):** Fed into my depression.
- **Belief(s):** Something bad is going to happen, but I don't know when.

- **Vow(s):** Something bad will always happen to me.
- **Comments:** This was like a heaviness or weight that came upon me. I would feel this often at bedtime while trying to say my bedtime prayers. Or, while having a fun time playing with my sisters or playing baseball, the anxiety would all of a sudden overwhelm me. I would just push it away.

21. Fear.
- **Situation/Event Causing Issue:** Did not grow up in a secure environment; father's beatings and his presence; mother's sickness—I had to take care of home as she might die; was not living like church said I should live; telling David my secrets; sexual abuse.
- **Effect(s):** Shame and guilt for feeling afraid; convinced father did not like, love, nor want me; pushed God away; uncomfortable with teens at youth group and did not go much.
- **Belief(s):** God will not let me get away with this. He will certainly punish me. I will not go to heaven. God is far away.
- **Vow(s):** Something bad will always happen to me.
- **Comments:** I can relate to anyone who has actually become "frozen" in fear as I experienced that in my sexual abuse. And the fears I felt before and during a beating also froze me. It is horrible.

22. Anger.
- **Situation/Event Causing Issue:** My father not being a father to me; father beating me; father being an adulterer; mother's sickness; having to be in charge of the home; our family did not function like other Amish families; man in my father's shop; seven molesters; parents did not protect me; God did not protect me or give me a healthy father and mother.
- **Effect(s):** Emotional problems; health issues.
- **Belief(s):** God is in no way who people said He was because of the things He allowed to happen to me.

- **Vow(s):** I will be sick forever. I will always feel angry.
- **Comments:** I had a lot of anger and I never expressed it in the right way. I held it in most of the time. However, after I was married, I would spill it out onto David after I got tired of holding it inside of me. When I was really sick, expressing my anger would take the little bit of energy I had right out of me. After David and I were in counseling, we started to practice the principle of Ephesians 4:26 wherein Paul tells us to not let the sun go down upon our wrath.

23. Humiliation/shame.

- **Situation/Event Causing Issue:** Beatings; growing up in a dysfunctional family; participating in all my sexual abuse; my secrets; being mocked; inviting a boy to touch me; feelings towards parents; father's adulterous behaviors; mother's depression and inability to function; my own behaviors; not living up to people's expectations of who I was supposed to be as a Lapp because my father was so well-known; joining church for the wrong reasons; not living up to the church's expectations; our dysfunctional family when I was so sick.
- **Effect(s):** I felt less of a person; I did not feel normal; I felt like the dirtiest Amish girl that ever lived; I felt like an unfit wife and mother.
- **Belief(s):** I am less of a person. I am a bad person. I am different. I am not normal. I am the dirtiest Amish girl that ever lived. I am an unfit wife and mother. I cannot be loved because I am too dirty.
- **Vow(s):** I will always be dirty.
- **Comments:** It took me a long time, but I did finally learn that the abuse was not my fault. And I came to understand that I had nothing to do with my parents' problems and issues. I came to learn that Jesus is all about taking care of my shame. He bore it on the cross. He took it from me. The discussions Elaine and I had about

this caused me to sense God's work in my life in a powerful way.

24. Guilt.

- **Situation/Event Causing Issue:** For my participation in the sexual abuse; for not fighting off my abuser when he had sex with me; being mocked; for inviting a boy to touch me; my secrets; not living up to people's expectations of who I was supposed to be as a Lapp because my father was so well-known; joining church for the wrong reasons; not living up to the church's expectations; our dysfunctional family when I was so sick.
- **Effect(s):** Depression.
- **Belief(s):** I do a lot of wrong and stupid things. God will get me.
- **Vow(s):** I won't live up to what people think a Lapp is. I won't live up to how the church says I should live
- **Comments:** I knew enough that God sees everything and He saw what I was doing so I felt really guilty, especially after I was mocked. I felt deeply guilty and it was a dirty guilt. I would push it away. God, why did you let this happen to me? Praying with Diane helped me with the guilt.

25. Neglected/showed no attention.

- **Situation/Event Causing Issue:** Parents gave no attention to me; being oldest child of six children.
- **Effect(s):** Deep feelings of insecurity; resentment; anger; I received attention from the man in my father's shop; lied to get David's attention.
- **Belief(s):** I am different from other girls who did get attention.
- **Vow(s):** I will get attention from the man in my father's shop.
- **Comments:** Even though family times were not a priority with my parents, I felt even more neglected as the births of all my siblings took their attention away from me. Children have basic needs and God designed the family as a place

where those needs should be met. When the family fails to provide those needs, children will look elsewhere for them to be fulfilled.

26. Poor self-image.

- **Situation/Event Causing Issue:** The environment and events of my whole childhood.
- **Effect(s):** I felt dirty and filthy, just like trash.
- **Belief(s):** I am dirty. I am filthy. I am trash. I am not a right person. I am unworthy. I am not good enough for God. He does not want anything to do with me.
- **Vow(s):** I will always be trash.
- **Comments:** As I received healing, the lies with all of their pain left. Now I feel strong. I feel good about myself. I see myself as God sees me—pure, holy, forgiven, and clean.

27. Unfair.

- **Situation/Event Causing Issue:** Why was I beaten the most; why, as a family, our family did not do family events together; my father not taking me places with him; as an adult, why did I have to be sick for so long, causing so much dysfunction in our family.
- **Effect(s):** Anger; loneliness; shame.
- **Belief(s):** My parents were very unfair. God is unfair and will always be unfair to me.
- **Comments:** I had to learn to accept what God allowed in my life and forgive where forgiveness needed to be granted. We need to learn that God is always fair, good, and just.

28. Left out.

- **Situation/Event Causing Issue:** When it seemed that everyone but me knew that my mother was having a baby; when my mother pleaded with my father for me to go with him on a trip, but he said no.
- **Effect(s):** Felt unwanted; loneliness; anger; humiliation; unloved.
- **Belief(s):** I am not wanted. Something is wrong with me. No one loves me.
- **Comments:** Although I talked this out with Elaine, these feelings really lifted when I saw

David taking our children with him to different places. I was glad that they received what I did not receive.

29. Used/taken for granted.

- **Situation/Event Causing Issue:** Men who sexually abused me; my father while working in his shop; my father when cutting his hair; having to run the home when my mother was sick and father was never around.
- **Effect(s):** Anger; shame; anxiety.
- **Belief(s):** I am trash. The only thing I am good for is to be their servant. The only thing I am good for is to be used by a man.
- **Vow(s):** If I ever have children, I will never use them as my parents used me.

30. Being a "side pleasure" for men.

- **Situation/Event Causing Issue:** Men who sexually abused me.
- **Effect(s):** Anger; shame; anxiety.
- **Belief(s):** I am trash.

31. Forgiveness.

- **Situation/Event Causing Issue:** The treatment and wrong-doing of my father, my mother, and my abusers. Myself for holding onto natural reactions to painful situations as they became sinful.
- **Effect(s):** Resentment; anger; bitterness.
- **Belief(s):** I have a right to feel the way I do because of what they did. No one will take that away from me. I do not have to feel guilty for feeling this way. I cannot forgive my father. I cannot forgive my abusers. I cannot forgive myself.
- **Vow(s):** I will never forgive my father. I will never forgive the man in my father's shop who abused me. I will never forgive my abusers. I will never forgive myself.
- **Comments:** It was hard. Dan, who counseled David and sometimes David and I together, taught me, however, that if I would put myself in a position of humility, God would show me things I needed to know in order to heal. God

had to bring me to a point that I was ready to
forgive. I had to know and understand what I
was forgiving. When I did that, I could forgive.

- **My father.** I had been dealing with unforgiveness towards my father before my neck surgery.
I came to realize that if I wanted to be forgiven,
I needed to forgive my father. A week before I
went into surgery, I forgave my father. Right
before I went into surgery, Dan asked me what
I would want to say to my father if he was still
alive. It was a good question to ask me because
there is always the risk of dying when you go
into surgery. What was in my heart at that time
was to tell my father, "I love you." God has done
a great work of forgiveness in me.
- **My mother.** Although the time before my
mother's death helped our relationship heal, I
still had to go there, in counseling, to deal with
my anger and unforgiveness towards her for
suggesting the beatings.
- **My abusers.** I had to forgive the men for using
me and taking advantage of me and my innocence. I realized that I would not heal if I did
not forgive them.
- **Myself.** It was hardest to forgive myself.

**32. How could God love me after what I did and what
I let happen?**

- **Situation/Event Causing Issue:** I participated
in and enjoyed the feelings I received when I
was touched sexually.
- **Effect(s):** Shame; dirty; unlovable.
- **Belief(s):** God does not love me. God can't love
me.
- **Vow(s):** God will never love me.
- **Comments:** Over a period of time I came to realize that love is what God is all about. He loves
me no matter what I do or do not do. That real-
ization came through counseling, my relationship with David, reading devotional books, and
reading the Bible on my own.

33. How could I talk to God when I felt so trashy?

- **Situation/Event Causing Issue:** The environ-

ment and events of my whole childhood caused me to feel this way.
- *Effect(s):* I felt unworthy.
- *Belief(s):* I cannot talk to God.
- *Vow(s):* I will just think about Him as He will not listen to me anyway.
- *Comments:* I felt shame and guilt when I would pray my bedtime prayers, wanting only to hide from God. Counseling with Elaine helped me to see God differently and praying with her helped me to learn how to talk to Him.

34. God was cold and distant.
- *Situation/Event Causing Issue:* My relationship with both my father and church was cold and distant.
- *Effect(s):* No sense of spirituality or relationship with God.
- *Belief(s):* God was too distant. I could not have a relationship with Him. If I just follow the rules of the Amish church I will be okay.
- *Vow(s):* I will obey all the rules so God will love and accept me.
- *Comments:* This changed little by little as I received healing. God is anything but cold and distant now. He is real and personal to me.

35. Cycles of sickness starting in childhood.
- *Situation/Event Causing Issue:* Started shortly after the sexual abuse started.
- *Effect(s):* I did not feel like a normal child.
- *Belief(s):* I am not normal. I can get attention if I am different.
- *Vow(s):* I will always be sick.
- *Comments:* I cannot remember exactly when these cycles of childhood sickness stopped, but I know that they stopped by the time I finished school. However, cycles of sickness have continued throughout my adulthood.

36. God was punishing me by making me sick as an adult.
- *Situation/Event Causing Issue:* I was sick for over 23 years.
- *Effect(s):* Anger at God.

- **Belief(s):** I deserved to be punished by God for what I was involved with in my father's shop.
- **Comments:** I learned that the beatings which damaged my sacrum and the pushing away of my memories and feelings are what actually made me sick.

37. Perfectionism.

- **Situation/Event Causing Issue:** Work in my father's shop had to be perfect; both parents were perfectionists.
- **Effect(s):** Frustration and anger when things were not done perfectly.
- **Belief(s):** I had to do everything perfectly. David had to do things perfectly. My children had to do things perfectly.
- **Vow(s):** I will do everything perfectly.
- **Comments:** Over the years I learned that things do not have to be perfect. Cleaning can wait. Even if David does not do things around the home like I would want them done, that is okay because I know that he has done his best.

38. Generational depression/lack of function ability.

- **Situation/Event Causing Issue:** My mother's mother and my mother both suffered from depressions, experiencing emotional breakdowns that caused an inability to function in life; my father also suffered from an emotional breakdown before he married my mother.
- **Effect(s):** I suffered from long-term, deep depression, making me not able to function in life.
- **Belief(s):** I am like my mother.
- **Vow(s):** I will do anything and everything I can so I do not end up like my mother.
- **Comments:** My grandmother and mother were both put on medication for their emotional problems because they thought that was the answer. Although I was first put on medication for depression, I know that healing came when I addressed all my stuffed memories and emotions.

39. My own sin.

- **Situation/Event Causing Issue:** My natural reactions to the abuse became groundwork for

sin in my life.
- **Effect(s):** Because it was not dealt with for all those years, I stayed emotionally, mentally, spiritually, and physically sick.
- **Belief(s):** I am messed up because of other people.
- **Comments:** All the abuse I suffered caused normal emotional turmoil such as anger, unforgiveness, guilt, shame, confusion, etc. However, as time went on, this normal emotional turmoil became my sin. Not until I entered counseling did I finally own my anger and emotional turmoil and deal with it as sin. That brought healing.

40. Why did no one tell me about sex?
- **Situation/Event Causing Issue:** No one told me about sex.
- **Effect(s):** It put me at a higher risk to learn the wrong way from someone who should have not taught me.
- **Belief(s):** Don't talk about sex. If I talk about sex I will feel dirty and full of shame.
- **Vow(s):** I will teach my children about sex.
- **Comments:** If I had been told about sex in a healthy and mature way by a healthy and mature adult, I may have handled the man in my father's shop differently as well as the boys and men who molested me.

41. The secrecy of sex/pregnancy.
- **Situation/Event Causing Issue:** People never talked about sex nor did women tell anyone if they were pregnant.
- **Effect(s):** Shame and guilt was attached to the subject of sex and pregnancy.
- **Belief(s):** No one should know if someone is pregnant.
- **Comments:** I have learned and now believe that a married woman getting pregnant should be a time of great joy not a secret. Life is given by God and a reason to rejoice. Sex implies a different level and type of intimacy. God designed it and there should be no shame attached to it.

42. Rare to have any special family times together.
- **Situation/Event Causing Issue:** We rarely spent time together.
- **Effect(s):** Felt like an outcast; shame.
- **Belief(s):** Our family is not normal. Our family is different.
- **Vow(s):** When I get married our family will do things together.
- **Comments:** I often wondered what was wrong with my parents.

43. Having to run the home at such a young age.
- **Situation/Event Causing Issue:** Because my mother was sick during much of my childhood, I often had to run the home.
- **Effect(s):** Resentment; anger; shame.
- **Belief(s):** All I am good for is work.
- **Vow(s):** If I ever get married, our children will never have to run our home.
- **Comments:** Because of my sickness, our children did have great and wrong responsibility within our home.

44. Joining church with wrong motives.
- **Situation/Event Causing Issue:** I joined church so my father's beatings would stop and out of obedience to my parents.
- **Effect(s):** Joy that the beatings would stop; was not sincere about church life or God.
- **Belief(s):** I had to join church because it was expected.
- **Comments:** I wish my parents would have been more involved in explaining church to me. Only the ministers explained it in our classes, but there was no life or power in their teachings. That is how I felt given my age and background at that time.

What I have shared are the negative and wrong events in my life that caused certain effects, beliefs, vows, and issues. I hope you noticed that some vows were good vows. Most people experience some degree of positive events in their life which also affect them.

I had positive experiences in my life. For me, however, the negative and wrong situations and events I
experienced affected me so deeply that they took away
my life. There are times when good things can come
out of a hard experience, so I have listed some of those
below.

1. **Situation/Event Causing Positive Influence:**
   Doing a good job at helping to make and restore
   carriages.
   - **Effect(s):** I felt some sense of self-worth.
   - **Belief(s):** Sometimes I can do good.
   - **Comments:** I believe that sense of self-worth
     carried me into my relationship with David and
     our marriage.
2. **Situation/Event Causing Positive Influence:**
   Grandfather trusting me to drive his sleighs.
   - **Effect(s):** I felt accepted as a granddaughter.
   - **Belief(s):** Grandparents are more accepting.
3. **Situation/Event Causing Positive Influence:**
   Having to run our home at a young age.
   - **Effect(s):** By the time I was married I had great
     experience in knowing how to run a home.
   - **Belief(s):** I was good at running a home.
4. **Situation/Event Causing Positive Influence:**
   Getting unreasonable beatings.
   - **Effect(s):** I was deeply hurt.
   - **Belief(s):** Children should not be beat.
   - **Vow(s):** I will never beat my children.

I trust this chapter has not only helped you
understand how I was affected in the long-term, but
that it can help you sort out the hard and difficult
times you have experienced in your own life.

What I Want to Tell You

You have heard my life story of my healing journey. And you have heard how the events and situations of my life affected me. I now want to share practical suggestions about life and relationships.

1. It is important for me to say that I did not share any of these events to stir up and/or glorify sin or Satan. In fact, it was very hard for me to share what I shared. But I share my story because all kinds of family dysfunction and sexual misconduct occurs within every culture, whether English or Amish. Many people think that the Amish culture as a whole is a very godly culture, but we have sin problems and abuse each other just like people in other cultures. It is wrong. These misconducts need to be brought to light so that parents, teens, and children in the Amish culture can be taught what is wrong and what is right.

2. If you do not understand or know how to deal with your feelings and emotions, please take steps to understand and deal with them. God not only created them, but He has them too. They are, therefore, important. Find a friend or friends you can talk with who can help you understand your emotions and deal with them.

3. If, when you read this book, you realize that you need healing, please be willing to travel this journey of healing. Go to counseling if you need to go. If your children need to go, encourage and help them to go. There is nothing wrong with counseling. It helped me tremendously.

4. I started my healing journey because I wanted a different life. What kept me going was that I wanted to continue to experience more and more victory. Nevertheless, there were two very difficult things for me: one was to humble myself when I saw something that needed to be changed, and the second was finding the strength to continually deal with hopelessness. I know that my healing journey will not be finished until I reach heaven's doors. If you start this healing journey, find the courage to walk over those pebbles that will hold you back from continuing your journey.

5. Let children express what they feel no matter how silly it may seem to you. They need to learn the value of expressing their feelings and emotions. And they need to learn how to handle them. Do not tell them to stop crying, but let them cry if they need to cry. Their feelings are real and at times very big to them, so do not minimize what they are feeling.

6. Tell your secrets to a trusted friend or a counselor. Pray together about it.

7. Please do not be ashamed if you have been diagnosed with mental illness or dissociation as you will learn about in the last chapter of this book. Just get help.

8. Make sure to explain to your children the changes their body will go through as they mature into adulthood.

9. Please tell your children about sex and where babies come from. If you do not tell them, they may learn about sex in a "dirty" way, giving them wrong ideas about sex and sexual things.

Christian bookstores sell books explaining sex to children. Buy one to help explain sex to them. Talk freely with them about the subject of sex so an environment of openness is developed.

10. Explain to your children how wrong it is for people to touch their body where a bathing suit should cover. Tell your children to let you or someone else in your family know if anyone touches their body in those places.

11. Hug your children everyday, and tell them that you love them.

12. Notice the special unique ways and talents about each of your children and tell each one what you see in him or her. Encourage them to keep being special in those ways and talents.

13. Please do not beat your children. Discipline them. When you discipline them, explain what they did wrong. Explain that they are being disciplined because their actions were wrong, not because they are bad.

14. Grow spiritually by going to Bible studies or support groups. Join a prayer group. There is tremendous power in a group setting.

15. Read Bible stories to your children and talk about how the lessons from those stories can help them in their daily life.

16. Learn what the Bible says about the Holy Spirit. As a Christian, He lives inside of you to lead and guide you. Teach your children about the Holy Spirit who lives inside of them when they become a Christian.

17. I earlier stated that when I met David I "had no idea how God was going to use David in my life." As you have read my story, I hope you could see the truth to that statement. My relationship with David was a key factor in my healing. In looking at the big picture of how David helped me, it happened in two major ways. First, he heard, listened, and accepted me as I told him all the details of why I felt "dirtier than the dirtiest trash can." He gave me that safe environment that I needed to bare my burdened heart. Second, he humbly took up the responsibilities at home that I could not do. Although we had our moments, overall he did all this with a loving and gentle spirit. I can never thank God enough for giving me a husband like David. May I suggest that if you have a sensitive spouse like me, share your story no matter how shameful, guilty, and hurt, you feel. However, if your spouse is not sensitive to your needs, pray and get a few trusted friends to pray that he or she would become sensitive to your hurts and needs. God's design in marriage is for complete intimacy and that intimacy begins with deep honesty and exposure.

The following are some comments from David concerning what he went through during our many difficult years.

> *When I married Naomi, I stood before God and made a vow to love and support her in sickness and health until one of us parted from this earth. I not only wanted to keep that vow, but I wanted to please God in the way I kept that vow. There were many, many difficult days, but I always felt that I needed to treat Naomi as Jesus would have*

treated her. At times Naomi needed my silent strength of love, support, and encouragement. For example, the times I just listened to her or I read to her. Then there were times when she needed a bold strength that pushed her beyond what she thought she could do. For example, the time she did not want to go for the second anointing. I felt compelled to make her go.

In spite of our mounting financial bills over the years, I learned to watch God provide for us. In a nutshell, I really wish Naomi would have told her secrets to me years before. Marriage should be that safe place for a man and woman to bare their soul to each other with unconditional love. As Naomi and I have done that through her unfolding story, God has blessed us in many ways.

I have learned much in my life, and I certainly have a lot more to learn. But as my mountain is being moved and even removed through my jagged-edged pebbles becoming smooth, I was and am able to clearly see my Father in heaven and grow through the power of His Holy Spirit. I want the same for you. For this reason, I had this book written.

The next two chapters, which are the last chapters, have been written solely by Linda to give a broader view of healing and the healing journey. It explains and shares options someone has in the healing journey. What she writes may not be embraced by everyone reading this book. However, I challenge you to consider and be open to all that she shares.

PAIN
and Its Source of Healing

PAIN . . . we heard about Naomi's pain. We can also **hear** it in the bloodcurdling cry of a little boy falling out of a tree, **see** it in the reddened faces of those leaving a funeral, **sense** it in the empty and distant eyes that are masked by the psychiatric world of medicine, **sympathize** with it when we hear of the man who lost both his multi-million dollar business and his unborn child to a miscarriage, **empathize** with it when we meet someone who is experiencing our same pain, and **discern** its roots as the driving force in one whose life is characterized by addiction and being incarcerated in prison.

And, whether or not we like it, every single one of us **experiences** pain in some form and degree during our lifetime. In fact, many of us like Naomi, **live out our childhood pain every single day of our lives** instead of allowing it to be the driving force to take us to the healing heart of God.

In learning about the heart of this miraculous God of the Bible who heals, we cannot escape facing the reality of pain and brokenness as described from Genesis 3 to Revelation 20. In fact, the events and truths of the Bible are a mirror into our own hearts. Let's find out how.

In Genesis 1:26-28; 2:7,18-25 we learn that God created Adam and Eve in His image. In chapter 1 verse 31 it says, "And God saw all that He had made, and behold, **it was very good** . . ." We learn in this verse that God was pleased with all He created.

Let's take a moment and put on our "wonder" caps. Do you ever wonder how Adam and Eve actually had a relationship with God? How did it actually work itself out? Did God talk directly to them from Heaven? Or did He speak to them merely through their spirits?

I think God was physically present in some form in the Garden of Eden since Genesis 3:8 refers to His ". . . presence. . . ." Genesis 2:15 says ". . . the LORD God took the man and put him into the Garden of Eden . . ." It seems to me that if He "took" Adam to the garden, He must have been present and walked him there. Genesis 3:8 even states that Adam and Eve ". . . heard the sound of the Lord God walking in the Garden. . . ."

I wonder how God walked, if He did walk with them. Did He walk fast or slow? What was His bodily form? What did His voice sound like as He talked? Did the three of them laugh together? What was their joy level like?

I am sure they had peace being together, but what did they talk about? Did they run? What fun things did they do together? Did they throw around coconuts and cantaloupes? They surely loved each other deeply and purely. Since they could eat from just about every tree in the Garden, what were their meals like? Did God eat with them? Did they sit down to eat or just eat along the way?

Take a moment and wonder a bit more. Maybe Adam and Eve learned about heaven from God. Maybe God told them about eternity in the past. Or maybe He told them about His Son, Jesus, and the powerful Holy Spirit. Did He have to teach them how to "live life" since they had no parents? Did they ask God the details about how He created Adam from dust and Eve from Adam's rib? Did God teach them to sing?

Who really knows how it all worked in the Garden except God, Adam, and Eve? The Bible is not clear concerning how their relationship actually worked itself out, but we do know that Adam and Eve did have a relationship with their Creator. They knew nothing else but a right, pure, honest, and open relationship not only with God, but with each other. They knew each other in a very healthy and intimate way. And God's presence was real, strong, and very personal.

God created Adam with three parts: a spirit, soul, and body. We were created in that same way. We have a **spirit** to give us an awareness of God. Through our God-given ability to fellowship, have communion and worship, we not only become aware of God but we can have a personal relationship with Him. This is where God's spirit, the Holy Spirit, is to live, speaking to, and leading His creations. Our **soul** brings awareness about ourselves. It is made up of our mind, our emotions, and our will. God desired that our soul would respond to the Holy Spirit's speaking and leading in our spirit. And lastly, our **body** brings about our awareness of the world around us and is very influenced by the temptations of the world. We can easily see that part. So God created man to live and function in life by listening to the Holy Spirit in his spirit.

Chapter 3 of Genesis shares the life-changing consequences to Adam and Eve's spirit, soul, and body because they listened to and were influenced by someone other than their very own Creator. As they listened to the serpent (Satan), they embraced his lies. This caused them to disobey. Immediately upon that disobedience, they changed. Among other qualities, the joy, peace, and pure love they experienced were no longer present. Instead, shame, fear, guilt, the blame game, and even more, immediately settled into their **soul**, causing the awareness of themselves to become dreadful. In addition, deadness immediately settled into their **spirit**, causing God's presence to be shut out. They no longer had an open relationship with God. Lastly, their **bodies** immediately sensed an environment affected by sin, causing them to hide from God. Although their bodies were separated from God by hiding, they also became separated from Him in their relationship. This happened because their souls and spirits became sinful.

Their soul spoke louder than their spirit because God's presence was shut out of their spirit. Unfortunately, their open and honest relationship with God ended and a relationship with sin started.

Habakkuk 1:13 says, "Thine eyes are too pure to approve [look at] evil . . ." We learn from this verse that God cannot even look on sin let alone be involved with it in any way. Because God has no sin in Him, He has to separate Himself from anything or anyone that has sin.

Can you remember a time when you did something wrong to a friend? Think about how you and your friend felt separated from one another. You felt separated because you were actually separated. The wrong doing or sin is what separated you. That separation caused an experience of hard and hurtful feelings between the two of you. You stayed away from each other. You did not talk. The situation between God and His creations was similar. Because of sin, Adam and Eve were now separated from their Creator, their Friend. They also became separated from each other. And God sent them out from the Garden of Eden. All this separation caused pain— deep pain. Pain was now borne into the human race.

Wonder for a moment about the horror that Adam and Eve experienced. One moment they lived in total purity and security, having absolutely no selfish, sinful, or dreadful thoughts and feelings, enjoying complete freedom to talk about anything and everything, not only to each other but to the One who created them. Then, upon their disobedience, they immediately became stripped of those privileges and filled with something different, something new, something called pain. Only Adam and Eve knew that dread—the horror, the pain of falling from perfection into sin. Their human desires for food, sex, to love and be loved became self-centered and sinful. And I wonder how long it was after they were created that they made that dreadful decision, plunging them into sin. I cannot imagine the level of regret they felt because that one choice to sin totally changed their life and the direction of it!

Did you ever make an unwise or wrong decision(s) that totally changed your life or affected it in a negative way? You regret what you chose. You live day in and day out with that regret. How Naomi regrets letting that sexual abuse continue in her father's shop. How she wishes that she had told someone about her secrets. How she regrets that she told no one about her secrets.

The first thing that Adam and Eve did was to find a way to feel better about themselves. So they gathered fig leaves and sewed them together, making loin coverings. I would not be surprised if their gathering of fig leaves was done in a very frantic way to quickly cover their exposed body. I wonder how they sewed the fig leaves together without the invention of a needle and thread or a good 'ole Singer sewing machine. However they made their clothes, we can clearly see that making and putting on their own clothes was their way to make themselves feel better. It helped them deal with their shame and inadequacy. Even though they worked hard to make themselves feel better, they still hid from the One who created them, or at least they tried to hide.

Unfortunately, every person born after Adam and Eve inherited that sin and separation problem with all of its pain (Psalm 51:5; 58:3; Romans 5:12; 6:23). *Vines Expository Dictionary of Old and New Testament Words* defines sin as "a missing of the mark." We commit sin when we fall short of what God asks us to do, or to say it another way, we sin when we disobey God. Romans 3:23 says, "For all have sinned and come short of the glory of God."

Examples of sin are lying, stealing, holding unforgiveness in our heart, gossiping, fornication, adultery, cheating, murder, and more. These actions and behaviors separate us from God. And in God's plan, He declared that there would be a punishment and penalty for that sin. He called it death. Romans 6:23 says, "For the wages [pay] of sin is death . . ." Death in the Bible represents separation. One definition of death speaks of a separation from God while living here on earth. Another definition of death is living in Hell forever and ever in the pain of being separated from God.

Being separated from God, while living on this earth, brings pain because God created us with a spirit, soul, and body so we can live in a healthy and whole relationship with Him, our Creator. Living outside of that relationship is very painful. Instead of that pain driving us to find our Creator, our pain often drives us to find and design our own fig leaf coverings so we, like Adam and Eve, can attempt to hide our shortcomings and inadequacies.

Everyone has fig leaf coverings. What are your coverings? Are you always smiling, telling people you are fine while continually feeling empty, dead, and depressed on the inside? Do you work so hard and long that you never have time for God or for your family or to look at the issues in your life that cause you pain? Do you believe, like Naomi, that you will be okay as long as you push painful memories away? Do you blow up at people, in your anger, to keep them away for fear that they find out what you are really like? Do you just keep taking medicine without a **consideration** to get help to address the painful issues rooted deep in your soul which **may be** causing your anxiety and depression? Do you reject people before they reject you? Do you run to alcohol or street drugs to keep you numb from the pain of your life?

Like Naomi, do you seek attention in relationships that are not healthy? Are you closed to sharing with people how you really feel inside about situations that happened in your life? Do you have to do everything perfect, trying to hide your own imperfections? Do you gossip to make yourself feel better? Do you just "follow the rules" instead of following the Holy Spirit?

Like Adam and Eve, we all have fig leaf coverings, trying to numb the pain of being separated from our Creator, trying to numb the pain of living in sin. But our fig leaf coverings are not durable. The leaves eventually start to fall off, exposing and plunging us deeper into our pain. But hallelujah, God did something about this pain.

Our Source of Healing

In spite of man's sin, with its punishment and penalty, God had and still has a deep, passionate, unrelenting love for His creations. He never did and never will turn from His love. In fact, He could not turn from it. His love never changes; it never weakens; it never dies. God not only loves us in spite of our sin but He loves us **in** our sin. His love is the same whether we are living right or living wrong. He loves the gal struggling to stop prostituting her body to get money for that drug high, as much as the mature, Spirit-filled, godly minister. It is an amazing and unfathomable love that God has for us. He does not love us in this way so we take advantage of Him. He loves us in this way so we can receive, return, and give out His love.

Although God was offended by Adam and Eve's sin, as it was His standard and law they disobeyed

(Psalm 51:4), His love did not lessen. In fact, His love spoke louder and His love chose to do something about that sin. In His strong and compassionate Fatherly love, He was driven to bring His creations out of sin and back into a relationship with Him. He believed that His creations were worth saving, after all, He created them in His image (Genesis 1:26,27; Colossians 3:10). His plan was to forgive the sin which was separating them from Him. In fact, His plan was designed in a way that the forgiveness of sin would actually cleanse or remove the sin, allowing the relationship to be restored. According to *Vines Expository Dictionary of Old and New Testament Words*, for God to forgive meant God would "send forth, send away" sin. In sending sin away, it would no longer be present.

In His plan God declared that "without shedding of blood there is no forgiveness" (Hebrews 9:22). God was saying that sin would be forgiven when blood was shed. Why blood? Blood represents life (Leviticus 17:11). So in short God was saying that without the giving of a life, which would be the giving of blood through sacrifice, there would be and could be no forgiveness of sin. As recorded in the Old Testament of the Bible, it was the shedding of an animal's blood through sacrifice that satisfied God because that shedding **covered** man's sin. In their sin being covered, they could have a relationship with God.

However, God wanted to do more than cover man's sin. So this is what God did: He gave His one and only Son, Jesus Christ, to come to earth as a man and die on a cross so people could enter into a relationship with Him that would last throughout eternity (John 3:16). In shedding His blood, Jesus would take the punishment for sin once and for all, cleansing sin, not just covering it. We celebrate God sending His Son to this earth at the Christmas season.

Shortly before Jesus died on the cross, He was deeply betrayed by His friends, Peter and Judas. Although Jesus poured three years of His time and self into these two men, they chose to turn their backs and betray the very One who loved them no matter what (Matthew 26:47-56; 69-75; Mark 14:43-50; 66-72; Luke 22:47-62; John 18:1-11; 15-27). Have you ever been betrayed by a trusted friend or a parent? Have you felt the disappointment, the hurt, the anger, the rage of betrayal? Jesus knows what that is like.

When Jesus was 33 years old, before His actual death on the cross, His whole body was first beaten and tortured by people. Isaiah 53:5 says, "But He was **pierced** through. . . . He was **crushed** . . . and by His **scourging** . . ." Verse 7 says, "He was **oppressed** and He was **afflicted** . . ." Isaiah 50:6 says, "I gave My back to those who **strike Me**, And My cheeks to those who **pluck out the beard** . . ." A **crown of thorns** was placed upon His head (John 19:2). These verses, together with the events recorded in Matthew, Mark, Luke, and John, teach the torture Jesus' body experienced. Isaiah 52:14 says, ". . . So His appearance was **marred more than any other man**. And His form more than the sons of men." Jesus was physically tortured to the degree that people did not even recognize Him. It is hard to even imagine. Can you believe that? Did you ever experience the horror of being physically tortured? Did you get beat like Naomi? Was it a parent or a babysitter or someone who stole something from you in a darkened alley? Jesus surely knows what it is like to be beaten and tortured. He understands your pain.

While His blood was dripping down, nails were pounded through His hands and feet, nailing Him to a cross that was laying on the ground. The cross was lifted up as they cast lots for His clothes (John 19:23,24). Deep, excruciating pain visited every fiber and cell within Him. In the midst of this deep humili-ation, Mark 15:29 says, "And those passing by were **hurling abuse** at Him . . ." The Romans crucified people totally naked. Most likely, Jesus was treated the same way. So, there he was, naked in front of his mother, a few friends, and all those who were abus-ing Him. Has anyone ever stood and verbally abused you in front of other people in a cold and vulgar man-ner, humiliating you? Has your naked body been ex-posed in the midst of abuse, humiliating you beyond any other experience in your life? Were your clothes or other belongings ever taken from you in some hurt-ful or criminal way? He experienced the deep shame and humiliation that exposure brings. Jesus under-stands your pain.

After Jesus was on the cross for three hours, darkness came upon the earth for the next three hours (Matthew 27:45; Mark 15:33; Luke 23:44). It was during this time that God showed His wrath against sin, once and for all. As Jesus bore sin in His body, God's wrath was actually poured out on His one and only beloved Son. He poured out His wrath on His Son so it does not have to be poured out on you.

I Peter 2:24 says, "And He Himself **bore our sins in His body** on the cross . . ." And II Corinthians 5:21 says, "He made Him who knew no sin **to be sin** on our behalf . . ." Isaiah 53:4 says, "Surely our **griefs He Himself bore**; And our **sorrows He carried** . . ." Verse 6 of that same chapter says, "But the LORD has caused the **iniquity** [sin] **of us all to fall on Him**." And verse 11 says, ". . . And He will **bear their iniq-uities** [sin]." Hebrews 9:28a says, "so Christ also, having been offered once to **bear the sins** of many . . ." You see, as those verses teach, Jesus bore our sin in His body. That means He experienced and felt, within His spirit, soul, and body, your sin and my sin, in-cluding its effects. Jesus understands and can identify with sin. Like you, Jesus felt the heavy weight of guilt, shame, anxiety, betrayal, anger, fear, etc. He experienced the power of that horrible mental anguish and painful emotion that robs you of the peace and joy of life. He understands the racing thoughts, the gripping fear, the raging anger, the drive to rid yourself of guilt, and the shame that keeps you from getting help. He certainly understands what you go through when that anguish captures your whole being and, like Naomi, you cannot even get out of bed. He understands the desire for a quick fix of medication or alcohol or street drugs. He understands it all.

Jesus' death was deeply horrendous in the physical realm, the realm that people could see with their eyes. As people mockingly encouraged the torture, they watched blood ooze out of His skin and muscles. His skin even became torn off. Psalm 22:14,15 says, "I am poured out like water, And all my bones are out of joint; My heart is like wax; It is melted within me. My strength is dried up like a potsherd, And my tongue cleaves to my jaws; And Thou dost lay me in the dust of death." People watched Jesus pour out His life and then dry up. If you have ever been abused in any form, to the degree that you thought you were going to die, Jesus certainly understands.

But Jesus' death was even more horrendous in another realm, the spiritual realm. You see, while Jesus was bearing all of that painful sin in His body, God had to turn His back. Remember Habakkuk 1:13 which says, "Thine eyes are too pure to approve [look at] evil. . . ." God could not be a part of sin in any way, so like Adam and Eve, Jesus became separated from God. That is why Jesus cried from the cross, "'Eli, Eli, Lama Sabachthani?' That is, '**My God, My God, why hast Thou forsaken Me?**'" (Matthew 27:46; Mark 15:34). Jesus felt the deep and dreadful anguish of being forsaken because He was separated spiritually from His Father. That was the deepest pain

Jesus experienced as He was hanging on the cross. This was new for Him because He had never been separated from His Father in eternity past.

Like us, Jesus knows what it is like to be separated from God. In fact, He knows what it is like to be forsaken by His Father. Were you forsaken by your father or some other person who was supposed to take care of you? Did they just leave you? Even though death took a loved one from you, do you feel forsaken by them? Have you felt rejected? Have you ever felt like God left you and is nowhere to be found? Do your prayers seem like they go unheard and unanswered? Jesus understands.

Consider the amazing and humbling truth that Jesus died this horrendous and inhumane death when He did not even deserve it. Jesus did not deserve it because He had never committed one sin. II Corinthians 5:21 says, "He made **Him who knew no sin** to be sin on our behalf. . . ." I John 3:5b says, ". . . in Him there is **no sin**." Jesus chose to bear sin in His body and take the punishment for sin, causing forgiveness to be granted, so we do not have to receive that punishment and we can enter into a relationship with God. This is why He is called our Savior.

Jesus saved us from the punishment and penalty of sin. Stop for a moment. Consider, really consider what Jesus did for you. Has anyone else ever done this for you? Has anyone died for you in such a horrendous way so that you could live? Could anyone else ever do this for you? May this amazing, outrageous, indescribable and unfathomable act of love open your heart to receive all that God has for you.

In fact, you and I are the ones who deserve this punishment of death because as Romans 6:23 says, "For the wages [pay] of sin is death. . . ." But because God loves us, He extended His mercy. **Mercy is not getting what we deserve.** Here is an example of mercy. Have you or someone you know ever stood before a judge expecting to be sentenced to prison for five years because the law says one should be in prison for five years, yet the judge only gives a sentence of two years? If so, mercy is what the judge handed down. We deserve to be beaten, punished and sent to hell for our sin, but Jesus took that punishment instead. He was our Substitute. If we receive God's forgiveness, as we will talk about later, we will never receive what we deserve. Lamentations 3:22, 23 says, "The LORD's lovingkindness [mercy] indeed never ceases, For His compassions never fail. They are new every morning; Great is Thy faithfulness." God's mercy is always available to us.

So, while Jesus was receiving this injustice and abuse on our behalf, how was He reacting? Isaiah 53 gives a clear picture. Verse 7 says, ". . . Yet He did **not open His mouth**; Like a lamb that is led to slaughter, And like a sheep that is **silent before its shearers** so He **did not open His mouth**." Isaiah 50:6 says, ". . . I **did not cover** My face from humiliation and spitting." I Peter 2:23 says, "and while being reviled, He **did not revile in return**; while suffering, He **uttered no threats**, but **kept entrusting Himself to Him who judges righteously**." Jesus did not say one resisting or nasty word. Nor did He try to get away. He did not retaliate or curse or threaten anyone. He trusted His Father and His Father's ways. And He endured the deep pain (Hebrews 12:2). He only spoke words of life. In fact, from the cross, Jesus said, ". . . **Father, forgive them**; for they do not know what they are doing. . . ." (Luke 23:34).

In the hurts and pain of life, it has probably been very hard for you to trust God like Jesus did in the midst of His pain. Have you quickly forgiven people who hurt you? Have you kept right and godly attitudes in the midst of being hurt? Have you kept quiet like Jesus did, or kept secrets, maybe for reasons like Naomi had? Most likely, no one ever taught you, especially when you were a child, how to deal with your hurt. Without the help of other people and God, we usually do not react in a healthy and good way.

Now, are you ready for one more amazing, life-changing truth? Let's look at God's reaction to the torture and separation His Son was experiencing. Isaiah 53:10 says, "But the LORD was **pleased to crush Him, putting Him to grief** . . ." And verse 11 says, "As a result of the anguish of His soul, He will **see it and be satisfied. . . .**" When God saw His very own Son's blood being shed, taking the punishment for sin so sin could be cleansed and forgiven, **He was satisfied**. This English word, satisfied, is rooted in a Hebrew word which expresses the idea of being filled. God was, in essence, **filled** when He saw His Son dying. **His death was enough**. Only the sacrifice of a person without sin could satisfy God because God's holiness demanded holiness. The sacrifice of animals only **covered** sin so man could have a relationship with God. But the pure blood of sinless Jesus **cleansed** sin, removed sin once and for all. I John 1:7 says, ". . . the blood of Jesus His Son cleanses us from all sin." Only Jesus could have cleansed sin. This was God's plan and nothing else had to be done or could be done for man to have a relationship with God. The shedding of Jesus' blood was the only way; only the shedding of Jesus' blood satisfied God.

From a human point of view, it is extremely difficult to comprehend how God was pleased to crush His one and only Son. And how could He feel **satisfied** when watching His Son experience such anguish? Among other things, it shows me how much God loves His creations. I often wonder if that actual separation made it easier for God to carry out His plan. I also wonder what other emotions God felt and what thoughts He had as He watched His Son in such anguish. Although we do not know what God experienced, we do know that sin was being punished. Therefore, God was satisfied. This was all because of love, God's relentless love for you.

To this day, the only way you can have a personal relationship with God is to trust that the shedding of Jesus' blood forgives your sin. You cannot and do not have to do anything else to have a personal relationship with God.

Works will not bring you into a personal relationship with God. Going to church, dressing a certain way, praying, reading your Bible as a novel to gain information, giving up sinful practices and making promises to God will never remove sin. Only the blood of Jesus can wash away sin. And that is what satisfied God.

A beautiful hymn was written by Robert Lowry entitled, *Nothing but the Blood of Jesus*. The first verse says, "What can wash away my sin? Nothing but the blood of Jesus. What can make me whole again? Nothing but the blood of Jesus." And the chorus goes on to beautifully state, "Oh! Precious is the flow; That **makes me white as snow**; No other fount I know; Nothing but the blood of Jesus."

From all the hours of physical, emotional, mental, and spiritual pain, life was little by little leaving Jesus' body as He endured the punishment of sin. In His humanness, Jesus finally declared, ". . . It is finished! . . ." Jesus was saying that the penalty and punishment of sin was paid for. His work was done. Sin was forgiven by God. Sin was cleansed, not just covered as it was during the Old Testament times. Sin was put away (Hebrews 9:22). Sin no longer had to separate God from His beloved creations. In making this declaration, Jesus then gave up His spirit and died (John 19:30). In Peter teaching about Jesus' death, he refers to ". . . the agony of death . . ." (Acts 2:24). I wonder how agonizing it was for Jesus when He died. What did He actually experience in death?

After learning some detail of what Jesus experienced in His life and death on the cross, we can be sure that Jesus knows the pain of jagged-edged pebbles.

Jesus was then buried. He was put in a tomb and it was sealed (Matthew 27:57-66; Mark 15:42-47; Luke 23:50-56; John 19:38-42). His burial was proof of His death.

But Jesus did not stay dead! In loving Jesus and in considering all that He did for us, we can rejoice and have a party that He rose from the dead! The events are recorded in Matthew, Mark, Luke, and John. We celebrate this victorious event on Easter.

Although **sin**, **death**, and the **devil** are extremely powerful, not one of them had the victory in Jesus' life. Hallelujah that Jesus could not be held in their power! Romans 6:9 says, ". . . Christ, having been raised from the dead, is never to die again; **death no longer is master over Him**." Acts 2:24 says, ". . . putting an end to the agony of **death**, since it was **impossible for Him to be held in its power**." Hebrews 2:14 says, ". . . that through death He **might render powerless, him who had the power of death, that is, the devil**." Hebrew 9:26 says, ". . . He [Jesus] has been manifested to **put away sin** by the sacrifice of Himself." The agony of sin, death, and the devil could not keep Jesus down. No, He had the victory! Hallelujah! And His victory is forever.

Did you ever experience a time when you had victory over a bad habit, a wrong thinking pattern, a sinful action? Weren't you filled with the peace and the joy of the Holy Spirit? Didn't you feel good? Because of what Jesus did for you, you can have that same victory continually and with other issues.

Wow! Can you grasp the passionate and outrageous love God has for you? He sent His only Son to be your substitute taking the punishment of sin so you can have a relationship with Him and live with Him forever in Heaven instead of Hell. And Jesus agreed to take that punishment. Only a selfless, unconditional, and totally outrageous love could do that. God loves you. Jesus loves you. Do you understand how deeply they love you? In fact, God did not tell His creations to "get it right and then I will send my Son to die for you." No, His plan went into action while His magnificent creations were sinners. Romans 5:8 says, "But God demonstrates [shows] His own love toward us, in that **while we were yet sinners Christ died for us**."

You see, because of love, a plan for forgiveness was made and carried out so you can live in a personal relationship with the very One who created you while you live on earth and throughout eternity. But it is up to you to open your heart and receive that forgiveness. His forgiveness is a free gift that you receive by faith. That means you cannot actually see this gift, but you believe all that God and Jesus did for you as written in the Bible. Your Creator offers you this gift so you can live in a healthy and whole way. But you must receive it. It is an extremely unique, one of a kind gift because you can and will never receive any other gift that could save you from the penalty and punishment of sin.

Think of it this way. You have a friend in pain and you decide to give her a gift. To do this you think about what she would like or what would help her in her time of need. Whatever you decide, you want it to be to be personal, just for her. You create the gift. Maybe the creation of the gift cost you a lot of money and/or time, but you do not mind that because you love and care for your friend in a very deep way. You take the time to beautifully wrap the gift. You place the gift in your friend's hands with a big smile on your face and a deep love in your heart. Your friend quickly opens the gift and immediately feels warmth and joy because you had created it just for her. It helped the pain. Although that gift cost you something, it was free to your friend. Your friend only had to receive your gift. In receiving your gift, your friend received blessing in the midst of pain.

If you do not receive God's gift of forgiveness, you will never know His healing and you will never live in eternity with Him. You will live in Hell, separated from Him forever and ever. Let's take a moment and see what the Bible says about Hell. There is much we do **not** have to wonder about.

- Hell is a place prepared for the devil and his angels. Matthew 25:41
- Hell consists of fire (Matthew 5:22; 18:9) and that fire never goes out; the fire is eternal; the fire is not quenched. Matthew 25:41; Mark 9:43-48
- Hell is a place where even a worm cannot die. Mark 9:43-48
- Hell is a place of eternal punishment. Matthew 25:46
- Hell is a place where people are sentenced to. Matthew 23:33
- Hell is a place of torment and agony. Luke 16:19-31
- Hell is a place of darkness and judgment. II Peter 2:4
- Hell is a place where you cannot leave to go to heaven. Luke 16:19-31

Is this a place you want to live forever and ever? You will if you do not receive God's free gift of forgiveness. The fire will never go out, and you will never be able to leave. May I suggest that you read the story of the rich man and Lazarus in Luke 16:19-31, noted above, wherein the beggar begs for water to cool off his tongue, saying, "'. . . for I am in agony in this flame.'"

In short, God designed a gift to bring His creations out of the pain of sin and into peace and joy. That gift is called the gift of salvation. If you have never received this life-saving gift, why not receive it by faith today?

Please do not even go to bed tonight without considering all that Jesus did for you and without receiving His gift. Open your heart. Repent. Do not delay! There is no guarantee that you will wake up tomorrow morning. Or maybe you are not sure that you have ever received it. You can make sure right now. God prepared this special gift just for you. Do not reject it! How would you have felt if your friend would have rejected the special gift you created and gave to help in her pain? Below is a prayer you can pray.

Dear God: I confess that I, like Adam and Eve, have a sin problem. I confess that my sin separates me from you. I know that You love me and sent your Son, Jesus Christ, to be my substitute. I place my trust in what your Son, Jesus, did for me in dying on the cross, and I receive His forgiveness and accept Him as my personal Savior right now, today. Please lead me to people who can help me heal and grow in my relationship with you. Amen.

Praise God if you just received His gift or if you received it at another time. Now you can be assured that you are going to Heaven if you died today. You are now a Christian. You are now God's child. In being God's child, you have many privileges and benefits. As you travel on your journey of healing, you will come to learn about, understand and experience these privileges and benefits.

Let's finish the story of Jesus as there is much more to learn.

Forty days after He rose from the dead, He ascended back into Heaven from where He came (Acts

1:9-11), and He sat down at the right hand of His Father (Mark 16:19; Acts 2:33a; Ephesians 1:20; Colossians 3:1; Hebrews 1:3).

Even though sin was forgiven, the devil still tries to bother us. He accuses God's children before the Throne of God (Revelation 12:10). In short, he brings your sin to God's attention. In Revelation 12:10, he is referred to as the ". . . accuser of our brethren. . . ." But as Jesus is sitting at the right hand of the Father, He is interceding for you (Romans 8:34; Hebrews 7:25). That means Jesus, like an attorney, defends you, stating that He took the punishment for your sin and you do not, therefore, deserve punishment.

Please put on your wonder cap again. Take a moment and wonder what it was like for Jesus to return to Heaven after experiencing the agony of sin, death, and the devil. Was conversation in Heaven any different in light of Jesus' earthly experiences? Did love for each other deepen? Was that even possible? In light of Jesus being human and experiencing human sin and struggles, did His empathy deepen for His Father's creations? What did the angels think about all of it? Did their worship of the Savior become more passionate?

Ephesians 1:7 says, "In Him [Jesus], we have redemption through His blood, the **forgiveness of our trespasses** [sin]. . . ." (Colossians 1:14). God's creations were now forgiven and have the opportunity to enter into a very personal relationship with Him. Sin no longer has to separate them from God. In having this personal relationship with God, we can grow in our relationship with Him (Colossians 2:6,7).

And that horrendous pain, which comes in different forms and degrees, can be healed. It needs to be healed because it stops our growth as a person and our growth in the Lord. Isaiah 53:5 says ". . . And by His scourging **we are healed**." I Peter 2:24 says, ". . . by His wounds **you were healed**."

As soon as you confessed your sin and trusted in what Jesus did for you, the Holy Spirit came to live inside of you (John 14:16-31; 16:5-15; I Corinthians 2:12; Ephesians 1:13,14). He actually entered the spirit part of you, bringing His presence into you. His presence makes your spirit alive so you can have a relationship with Him. Remember it was said earlier that your spirit brings about a consciousness of God? Without the Holy Spirit in your spirit, your spirit is dead. But once the Holy Spirit enters your spirit, His presence will make you more and more conscious of God. Your relationship with Him can become personal and powerful. You can now go on and experience the mighty work and ministry of the Holy Spirit. God's intention is that we grow in the Spirit, continually experiencing His presence in deeper and fuller ways.

God's deep love and compassion moved Him to provide a way to save His creations from what they deserved—death. This was and is God's **mercy** at work on our behalf. Instead He gave them the opportunity to receive forgiveness and the many blessings that come with God's forgiveness. This was and is God's **grace** at work on our behalf.

Many people experience great relief at the moment of salvation. At that time, the Holy Spirit is real and they experience a hunger to learn about God and experience more and more of His presence in their lives. They continue to grow in the Lord and even experience a change in their behaviors. God becomes very personal to them. Then for some people, God, little by little, begins to become distant. They begin to experience a lot of negative feelings and express them to the world around them. God does not seem to be listening. The words of the Bible become dull. Faith seems to have no power, and all kinds of imma-ture, wrong and even sinful behaviors become a part of their daily life. They are stuck and not growing in the Lord.

Why? They often need to be healed from childhood hurts that are lodged in their soul. Like Naomi, there are a lot of jagged-edged pebbles, causing extreme pain and poison inside. Life can become extremely painful. Our Creator wants us to run to Him for comfort, for encouragement, for healing. He wants to dry our tears if they come easily. Or He wants to cause tears to flow if we vowed to never cry. Psalm 139:13 says, "For Thou didst **form my inward parts**; Thou didst **weave me in my mother's womb**." And verse 15 says, ". . . And **skillfully wrought** in the depths of the earth." God formed you, God weaved you, God skillfully wrought you. Those words teach that He designed and created every single part of you, your spirit, soul, and body. And it is He who gave you a personality. Since He did all that, He definitely knows you better than you even know yourself. God knows what makes you tick.

Also, Daniel 2:22 says, "It is He who reveals the profound and hidden things; **He knows what is in the darkness**, And the light dwells with Him." God not only knows the details of how you are made, but He knows your deepest sin. He knows your deepest need. He knows the detail of those horrid memories you have pushed away like Naomi, or forgotten, or just left behind. He desires to shine His healing light right into the painful darkness deep within you.

And God knows how you have dealt with your pain. He knows if you stuffed your feelings, if you spilled your feelings onto everyone around you, or if you dissociated, separating yourself from your feelings. God knows, He knows everything about you.

So why, like Adam and Eve, do you frantically put on your fig leaf coverings and run from the Spirit of this awesome Father and Creator? You don't have to run **from** Him. Run **to** Him. And keep running to Him. Never stop. When you fall down, get up and start running again. If you need help getting up, get help. But don't look back. Don't look to the sides. Don't listen to negative opinions and judgments of other people. Just look to the Holy Spirit and learn lessons from your falls. After all, through Jesus Christ, a way of healing and wholeness was provided for you. Those jagged-edged pebbles can become smooth, causing the pile to become smaller. As the pile becomes smaller, your mountain will move and you will see God clearly.

Your Healing Journey

Jesus loves me! This I know,
For the Bible tells me so;
Little ones to Him belong,
They are weak but He is strong.

Jesus loves me! He who died,
Heaven's gate to open wide;
He will wash away my sin,
Let His little child come in.

Jesus loves me! He will stay,
Close beside me all the way;
Thou hast bled and died for me,
I will henceforth live for Thee.

Chorus:
Yes, Jesus loves me!
Yes, Jesus loves me!
Yes, Jesus loves me!
The Bible tells me so.

"Jesus Loves Me" is a simple and very much loved tune written in 1860 by Anna Bartlett. She had written those words as a poem to be included in a novel that her sister, Susan, wrote. In that novel, this simple poem was read by a Mr. Linden as he was comforting a dying child, Johnny Fax. It has since become one of the favorite songs of children around the world. Yet it can minister just as profoundly to adults as it speaks of the amazing love of Jesus, the fascinating Son of God, who is the center of all the events and truths recorded in the Bible.

I refer to this man as fascinating because, before His death, while He walked this earth, He had the unique ability to humbly capture the attention of people in pain. People walked miles to see Him, people ran to see Him, people pushed through the crowds to see Him. The Bible speaks of hopeless individuals, desperate to receive the healing touch of this captivating Man everyone was talking about.

In looking at the powerful encounters Jesus had with people as recorded in the Bible, we see the unique and different ways that Jesus healed. For example, many times Jesus healed people who were possessed with a demon, merely through His commanding words (Matthew 8:16; Matthew 17:14-18; Mark 9:17-29; Luke 8:26-36). The lady who suffered from the issue of blood for 12 years was healed as she touched the edge of Jesus' cloak from behind. She merely placed faith in His healing power (Matthew 9:20-22; Mark 5:25-34; Luke 8:43-48). Jesus touched the eyes of two blind men and they could see (Matthew 9:27-31). He carefully placed clay on the eyes of another blind man and his sight was also restored (John 9:1-12). And another blind man could see after Jesus spit on his eyes and laid hands both on him and his eyes (Mark 8:22-26). Wow! Three different ways Jesus healed three blind men.

Bartimaeus' faith alone healed him (Mark 10:46-52; Luke 18:35-43). Jesus spoke over and laid hands on a lady who was bent over from an 18-year sickness (Luke 13:11-13). He touched the hands of Peter's mother-in-law and she was healed (Matthew 8:14,15; Mark 1:30,31; Luke 4:38,39). A mother's faith healed her daughter from being demon-possessed (Matthew 15:21-28). The paralytic, who was lowered through a roof, was healed because of the faith of those who took him to Jesus (Mark 2:1-12; Luke 5:18-26). And the man with a withered hand was healed merely through his obedience (Matthew 12:9-13; Mark 3:1-5; Luke 6:6-11). Jesus healed in many different ways through His miraculous healing powers.

As we learned in the last chapter, this same Lord Jesus Christ is the source of Naomi Stoltzfus' healing. She is getting healed in a way that is personally designed for her.

You heard Naomi's life story. Your life story is different than her story. Maybe your life was more difficult and painful than her life. Or maybe the events of your life were not as difficult to experience. You may be Old Order Amish like Naomi. Maybe you are Catholic. Maybe you are solidly engaged in the New Age culture. Or maybe you are sitting in jail or prison wondering if you and your life will ever change.

In reality, it does not matter who or what we belong to or how we identify ourselves. The bottom line is that, like Naomi, we all have jagged-edged pebbles causing pain that needs to be healed. And we have designed our own fig leaf coverings to cover up that pain. It is at that place of pain where we can meet Naomi. It is at that place of pain where we can meet Jesus and experience His life-changing ministry.

Like Naomi, you will have to look at the pebbles which grew your mountain. On your journey you will go up and down and all around that mountain. At times the terrain will be hard and difficult because the pain from the jagged edges of the pebbles may be very intense, seeming to give you greater pain. But the pain will lessen as those jagged-edge pebbles turn smooth through the healing power of Jesus.

So let's think once again about Adam and Eve. In reading Genesis 3:8-24, we learn that in the midst of their sin, God pursued them. Isn't that amazing? He cared enough to walk towards them as they hid (Genesis 3:8). He called them in their fear, asking them direct questions even though He knew that the blame game would be their response (Genesis 3:9,11,13). He cursed the serpent (Genesis 3:14,15). And although He declared consequences over their sin,

He replaced their fig leaf coverings with garments of skin (Genesis 3:16-19,21), as they are certainly a more durable and effective covering. Because God's love, mercy, and grace spoke louder, He pursued.

And God is pursuing you. He first pursued you to become His child. He will continue to pursue you in order to smooth your jagged-edged pebbles and replace your fig leaf coverings. Take a moment and think about why God would pursue you. Colossians 1:16 says, "For by Him all things were created, both in the heavens and on earth, visible and invisible, whether thrones or dominions, or rulers or authorities—**all** things have been created by Him and **for** Him."

Notice it says that everything was created by Him and for Him. How much is everything? Everything. It means all! And everything includes you. That means you, too, were created for Him. **You were created for God!** If God created you for Himself, would He treat you like an object and merely put you on a shelf to collect dust, with no purpose? No. God created you with a purpose in mind.

Isn't a cake created for the purpose of eating? Isn't a wooden table created to hold items? Isn't a business created for the purpose of helping people and making money? Nothing is ever created without a purpose. A creator always has a purpose for his creation. The same is true concerning God's creations. He created you with a specific purpose in mind. And *your* **purpose will be found when you are in a relationship with Him.**

As stated earlier, we enter into a relationship with God by confessing our sin and accepting Jesus as our Savior. When we do that the Holy Spirit enters into and lives in our spirit. That makes us God's child. That brings His presence within, causing us to grow spiritually. Spiritual growth happens through prayer, personal Bible study, being discipled and mentored, attending church and fellowship groups, and being involved in ministry. Spiritual growth causes our choices and behaviors to become like those of Jesus. Spiritual growth has a purpose: that we would grow to be more like Jesus in our attitudes, thoughts, and behaviors and as that happens we find and carry out God's purpose for us.

Yet as the prior chapter mentioned, many of us come to that place where we seem to no longer be growing spiritually. God seems distant. Our purpose in life seems to be drying up. Joy seems to be a memory of the past. That ugly and destructive anger starts spilling out on anyone who crosses our path. Fear returns. Depression sets in. These emotions are warning signs, signaling the existence, like Naomi, of some jagged-edged pebbles. When we see this happening, we need to realize that we need help; we need healing.

The following paragraphs offer some information about abuse and suggestions concerning how to travel on this life-long journey of healing. The purpose is to provide some direction for that journey. The information and suggestions may be overwhelming as there is much to read. If you begin to feel weighed down, only read the sections that would be important to you at the time you read. You can always process and digest the information and suggestions at a later time.

Purpose of Healing

Healing, just like spiritual growth, has a purpose. In healing you, God wants to restore in you what was lost in the Garden of Eden. Adam and Eve lived perfect, whole, healthy relationship and fellowship with God and each other. What was lost is what God wants to restore in you: relationship and fellowship with Him. In a nutshell, His presence in you is the key to your relationship and fellowship with

Him, the key to your becoming healed and whole.
What is Healing?

Many definitions of healing, including spiritual, emotional, mental, and physical, could be given. However, I think descriptions can help us better understand healing. Healing is happening when:

- You can think about a painful memory and experience peace instead of hurt.
- Some degree, if not all, of your anxiety and depression are replaced with a greater degree or even total peace and joy.
- An emotion like fear is replaced with peace, confidence, and trust.
- You meet a person who hurt and maybe even violated you and you do not well up with anger or rage.
- You experience freedom from addictions, i.e., drugs, alcohol, pornography, gambling, food, caffeine.
- Your body reacts in a more healthy way to stress.
- Prayer, worship, and reading the Bible are more alive and powerful.
- You come to know God's presence and voice in your spirit to a greater degree. Hence, you begin to live according to that still small voice speaking through your spirit instead of the dark and sinful thoughts, feelings and intentions of your soul.

Abuse and sin clog your spirit, soul, and body so you cannot have fellowship with God or hear from Him. God desperately wants to unclog what became clogged. In short, healing is happening when little by little you are living ore consistently and confidently according to the Holy Spirit's promptings and voice in your spirit. Healing is about the Holy Spirit bringing His presence, His touch of light into your darkness (Daniel 2:22; II Corinthians 4:6). In doing this you can experience the flow in relationship that Adam and Eve had with God and each other before sin.

Your healing is all about the Holy Spirit. The Holy Spirit is all about your healing. Encountering and experiencing His presence is the key.

If you have no idea what this means, read on. You can learn how to find the right kind of help so what is described above will become your daily experience. It will be very exciting as you learn to experience the presence and power of the Holy Spirit working in and through your spirit.

In the Beginning

As you begin your journey of healing, there are some important things I suggest you think about and try to remember.

1. Be careful that you **do not put God and how He works in a box**. He can heal you however He wants. Remember the unique and different ways that Jesus healed. Be open. God is healing in many different and miraculous ways around our globe through mighty movements of the Holy Spirit.

2. Be **willing to travel God's journey for you**. If you want healing God's way, He will certainly make that healing journey possible for you. Although it would be extremely helpful for you to talk with other people who are going through the healing journey, be careful that you do not follow the healing path of someone else. Seek God for your journey. Even if God does not seem to be real to you, pray and ask Him to show you the way. If God opens a door for you, pray about it. If you have peace to walk through it, trust God and walk through that open door. You may want to find a friend who you can talk to and pray with if you are not sure which way to go.

3. **Stick with your healing** no matter what. You may need to stop counseling for a period of time to "catch your breath." That is certainly understandable. However, determine to get back into it at some point.
4. **It does not matter what other people think.** If you want healing, go for it. Do not let anyone stop you.
5. As you are able, and if you desire, **attend healing services**. Put yourself in a place of belief, looking to God for Him to release His measure of healing upon you. And believe God for your healing, whether it is physical, emotional, mental, and/or spiritual, until He shows or does otherwise. Some healing may be immediate, some may be total, some may be partial. He may withhold some healing until another season of your life, or He may not give any measure of healing to some of your pain. God has purposes for healing and not healing His children. May I suggest that you merely be open for Him to heal you in whatever way He does or does not choose.

Important Things to Understand:

1. **Abuse.** Governments and agencies have come up with definitions and descriptions of abuse and they vary from state to state. However, the United States government has given a definition of child abuse. It is:
    "The physical or mental injury, sexual abuse or exploitation, negligent treatment, or maltreatment of a child under the age of 18, by a person who is responsible for the child's welfare, under circumstances which indicate that the child's health or welfare is harmed or threatened thereby." Child Abuse Prevention and Treatment Act, Public Law 93-247, 93rd United States Congress,

Senate 1191, 1974.

The Office for Victims of Crime, located in Washington, D.C., describes child abuse as follows:

"Child abuse is generally defined as any act or conduct that endangers or impairs a child's physical or emotional health or development. Child abuse includes any damage done to a child that cannot be reasonably explained and is often represented by an injury or series of injuries appearing to be intentional or deliberate in nature. Child abuse includes physical abuse, sexual abuse, emotional abuse, and neglect (which is the failure to provide a minimum standard of care for a child's physical and emotional needs)."

In short, abuse is any action towards someone that brings harm and damage. Those actions are not accidental, but deliberate. It is not just about child abuse. Adults, those 18 years of age and older, also experience abuse of many types, i.e., domestic violence, emotional abuse, sexual violence, financial abuse.

One type of abuse that is rarely mentioned and addressed in our culture is spiritual abuse. "Spiritual abuse, like all forms of abuse is a violation of God's standard in that it is a perversion of and/or failure to carry out God's heart of justice, mercy, grace, and love as taught in the Bible. Bible verses, truths and/or principles about God are distorted and/or used as a weapon against someone in order to manipulate, intimidate, dominate, control and/or degrade. It also includes inappropriate shunning and/or excommunication. Spiritual abuse puts water on the fire of the Holy Spirit. It causes one to develop a lie-based view of God, wherein a personal and fulfilling relationship with God is most difficult to attain. One spiritual abuse survivor described it as 'the Bible was used as a hammer to nail down my coffin.'" (Adapted for Wellspring Garden Ministries, Kinzers, Pennsylvania from REST Ministries' *Bridge to Restoration* notebook.)

2. **Abuse and sin.** The following points share the significant truths to help you understand the subject of abuse and sin:

- We all sin against one another, but when it endangers, impairs, and is non-accidental to another individual, it is abuse. It is harmful.
- This harm wounds and damages one's spirit, soul, and body. What hurts and wounds an individual are the lies, judgments, vows, and demonic activity that enter and lodge themselves in one's spirit, soul, and body. These cause emotional pain and that pain often becomes the driving force in one's life.
- Many times, a child who has been abused tells no one. That child is then left drowning in pain, whether or not it is acknowledged and felt to its fullest. Remember how Naomi thought she had no emotional pain? She had, however, just buried it. It was still there, destroying her emotional, spiritual, mental, and physical health.
- In short, abuse builds an ungodly foundation in one's life because abuse sets painful thoughts and feelings in motion. If no one is helping a wounded individual deal with their hurt, as one turns older, those painful thoughts and feelings can spring up as bitter roots, easily causing sinful behavior in one's life.
- That person needs to eventually own and deal with their behaviors as sin.
- This can be very hard to understand, but grasping it is extremely essential to one's healing. It may take a while to grasp, but that is okay. God will open one's eyes when the timing is

right.
- May I make an extremely careful point of caution. If you experienced hurt and trauma as a child, it may have affected how your brain, mind, and body function together, causing some kind and degree of mental health issues. Dealing with mental health issues as merely a sin problem, may cause even more damage to someone. It is essential that one finds a counselor that understands mental health issues.

3. **Long-term consequences of childhood abuse.** I trust that the chapter entitled "My Healing Journey" helped to bring understanding about how events of life affect us. In short, we experience and/or observe situations, both good and bad, and they affect us.

- We experience or watch a certain situation happening.
- We develop thoughts and feelings about that situation.
- We then develop a belief about God, others, and/or ourselves based on our thoughts and feelings.
- We develop certain patterns of thinking about people and situations.
- Sometimes we make a vow. A vow is a determination or declaration we make, based on a belief.
- Sometimes we make a judgment. A judgment is a decision we make and keep in our heart about someone or something.
- Sometimes we develop soul ties or bonds with people. A soul tie or bond is the invisible and powerful connection we have with someone that keeps us tied to them.
- Sometimes spirits are passed down from

generations before us or transferred from people we are involved with in specific situations. These spirits cause demonic activity in our lives.

- We carry those thoughts, feelings, emotions, beliefs, thinking patterns, vows, judgments, soul tie/bonds, and demonic activity with us throughout life. They can actually become the driving force in our life.

- Negative situations can cause negative affects, although it is possible for negative situations to teach us good things in life. That happened to Naomi.

- Positive situations can cause health and wholeness in our lives.

- Depending upon the type and degree of abuse and the person, one can leave their normal stream of consciousness during abuse. That means one can mentally focus on something else while they are being harmed. This is called dissociation because one actually dissociates or separates their mind from the pain. Although it is a God-given gift to help a child through pain and trauma, it can cause many problems later in life. There are many levels of dissociation.

4. **You.** You are you. God uniquely created you just the way He wanted you to be. Everything about you and your environment affected you while growing up.

- God gave you a specific **personality**. There are different types of personalities. Your personality may handle a certain type of abuse differently than another type of personality.

- The **environment** you grew up in had a lot to do with how situations and events affected you.

An environment is made up of the places and surroundings where you spent time and the attitudes and actions of the people who were in those places. If you grew up in a godly environment, your heart has godly truth and principles stored in it. Those truths and principles often affect many people for good during their healing journey. If, however, you grew up in a sinful environment, your heart will have to learn the truths and principles in the Bible. Maybe you grew up in an environment that had a bit of both. The significant point you need to understand is that what your ears heard and received into your soul and spirit and what your eyes saw and received into your soul and spirit affect you today.

- The **length** and **intensity** of your abuse had a great impact on the affect of your abuse. The longer and more intense your abuse was, the more harmful the affects.
- **Who** abused you will also greatly impact the affects of your abuse. The abuse of a father can have greater affects than a babysitter because of the expectations of the relationship.
- Proverbs 22:24-25 says, "Do not associate with a man given to anger, or go with a hot-tempered man, lest you learn his ways and find a snare for yourself." This verse supports how the people you associate with will affect you.

5. **Spirit, soul, and body.** There are various discussions and opinions about this subject. What is important to know is that, as already mentioned, God created man to live from His spirit. This means God wants you to know the voice and movements of the Holy Spirit's presence in you. Unfortunately, because of sin, we are very "soulish" people living

according to what our wounded mind, emotions, and will. People can be forcefully abused/tortured to a degree that they feel they have no will. Their will seems to not be their own. Our soul is often full of deep hurts, wounds, and sin. And our spirit is often very dull, and at times broken, remaining broken even after we become a Christian. Our bodies often bear the hurt through physical sickness and disease. All three need to be healed and delivered so our soul and body can be influenced by our spirit. Both healing and sspiritual growth help to cleanse the soul and enliven the spirit. As this happens, little by little you will experience a greater sense of the Holy Spirit's presence, promptings, and voice. This will bring you into a whole and healthy relationship with God. May I suggest that as you enter counseling, make this one of your goals: to learn how to hear clearly from the Holy Spirit. Life will take on a new direction and meaning when you live life hearing from the Holy Spirit.

Things That Will Come Against You During Your Healing Time

1. **The world system.** The world system is made up of all the systems set up in the world by people. Examples are advertisement, the media, marketing, entertainment, etc. Their purpose is to bring a greater degree of sustenance and comfort to people living in society. However, the result is that it often distracts people from God so they remain separated and independent of Him. People in the Amish culture are very good at being separated from this system. However, if you are not Amish, the invitations and offers of the world can keep you from the Lord. This system is not designed to draw you to the Lord.

2. **Your flesh.** Your flesh is not just the actual flesh on your body. It is your human nature which desires food, sex, happiness, to love and be loved. There is nothing wrong with these desires because God created desire and passion. However, if we do not learn how to bring these desires and passions under the control of the Holy Spirit, they will cause us to sin. These human desires, by themselves, only want to please self. James 1:13-16 teaches that the desire of your flesh, which is lust, is what tempts you to sin. And Romans 8:7 teaches that your flesh does not even have the ability to submit to God. Your flesh can only pull you away from God; it will not and cannot draw you to the Lord. And your flesh will be with you until you are in heaven. Great spiritual growth can happen in your life when you learn how to bring these desires and passions under the control of the Holy Spirit. The effects of abuse, however, can easily trap you to live according to your desires and passions instead of according to the way God designed you to live, through the presence, promptings, and voice of the Holy Spirit in your spirit.

3. **The devil.** The devil will do anything and everything to keep you from having a personal relationship with the Lord. He is a liar and the father of lies (John 8:44). That is his nature. The only mission he has is to steal, kill, and destroy (John 10:10). And the only tool the devil has to work with is a lie (John 8:44). It is amazing how he uses his lies. He tricks us into believing his lies to the point that his lies become our truth. By that I mean, we embrace his lies and live according to them. It is critically important that you recognize the lies you believe and how he tricks you or has tricked you to believe his lies. Naomi believed many lies as noted in the "Belief(s)" lines in the "My Healing Journey" chapter.

Your Work

1. **Obtain prayer warrior(s).** If you are taking deliberate steps towards healing, may I suggest that you ask a couple of people to be prayer warriors on your behalf. I say prayer warriors because the devil, your enemy, will never want you to be healed from your hurts and wounds. Think and pray about one or more persons who would faithfully lift you up before God in prayer; one who understands and will know how to war on your behalf. I am talking about a war in the spiritual realm, a war that you are in whether or not you realize it, a war that you cannot actually see. It is a war because the enemy and all his helpers will do anything and everything to keep you away from people and situations which will help you to heal. Make sure to keep in contact with your prayer warriors, telling them how you are doing. They do not need to know details unless you are comfortable sharing details. As mentioned earlier, if you are comfortable, you could ask their advice when you are not sure of the direction God is taking you.

2. **Receive counseling.** There are different types of counseling. It is, therefore, very important that you find a counselor with whom you are comfortable. There are lay counselors, biblical counselors, licensed counselors, professional counselors, pastoral counselors, psychologists, and psychiatrists. They often overlap in how they counsel.

   Before we look at the different types of counseling, may I state that regardless of what type of counseling you receive, relationship with your counselor will be a key factor to your healing. You will learn from your counselor and your counselor will learn from you.

~ **Cognitive counseling.** Cognitive counseling is counseling that happens within the realm of your mind. This kind of counseling is extremely important because it teaches you how to use your mind to "process" what happened to you. Remember how Naomi had to learn how to feel, how to know what it was she felt, and how to understand the affects of situations and events. Naomi was learning how to process the events of her life through her mind. That is what cognitive counseling does.

Within this realm of cognitive counseling, there is biblical counseling, where the verses, truths, promises, and principles of the Bible are discussed and applied to someone's situation. This counseling often exposes the lies that are believed and the sin that is being committed. Naomi shared situations which happened in her life and Elaine gave advice based on what the Bible taught. It was then up to Naomi to follow Elaine's biblical advice. That was life-changing for Naomi. It was in those sessions where Naomi learned how to process situations that happened in her life in light of what the Bible said.

The book of Proverbs speaks much of the value and need for counselors in our lives. People who counsel through using the Bible call themselves biblical counselors. There are different kinds of training one can go through to become a biblical counselor. Some are called lay counselors. Lay counselors do not have a college education, but have been trained to some degree by other groups to counsel from the Bible. Pastoral counselors are pastors who have been trained in college to counsel from the Bible. Anyone can benefit from biblical counseling.

Biblical counselors are found in churches, ministries or a biblical counseling center.

There is another form of counseling, within the realm of cognitive counseling, which is not needed by everyone. It is counseling for people who have experienced abuse to the degree that their brain, mind, and body, became overwhelmed because of pain and/or expected pain. In being overwhelmed, damage often happens to the brain, mind and body, including damage in how they function together. This counseling requires someone who has a very sensitive understanding of this type of damage. This type of counselor often works with a psychiatrist who can dispense medicine to assist in the healthy function of the brain, mind, and body.

We recommend that you find a counselor with this understanding who will also bring the principles of the Bible and the ministry of the Holy Spirit into helping the brain, mind, and body to work together. Counselors who are called professional or licensed usually have a greater understanding in this area. They are often psychologists because they studied psychology in college. These types of counselors can be found in churches and Christian ministries, but are mostly found in professional counseling centers.

God is, however, raising up lay and pastoral counselors, those without a college degree in psychology, who are being led by the Holy Spirit to understand the affects of abuse to the brain, mind, and body. These types of counselors are found in churches, Christian ministries, or biblical counseling centers.

~ **Prayer ministry.** Prayer ministry is also called inner healing counseling. Naomi experienced this in a powerful way. As explained earlier, in this type of counseling the Holy Spirit is the actual counselor as He takes people to memories where first-time hurt and trauma were experienced. As Diane prayed, the Holy Spirit led Naomi into painful memories. Upon visitation to that memory, specific thoughts, beliefs, vows, and feelings were dealt with and resolved by the Holy Spirit.

There are many ways that the Holy Spirit resolves conflicts, but He does resolve them and gives peace where once there was pain. The significance of prayer ministry is that it usually brings quicker healing to painful memories. John 16:13a says, "But when He the Spirit of truth, comes, He will guide you into all the truth. . . ." And John 14:17 and 15:26 refer to the Holy Spirit as the ". . . Spirit of truth . . ." This teaches us that the Holy Spirit will show us the truth beneath our emotional turmoil, the truth lying in the darkness. At times healing does not happen right away because there may be issues blocking the healing. The person leading in prayer ministry needs to know how to handle those blocks. There is training available for this type of healing. Any kind of counselor can be trained in this type of counseling, but not all counselors have the ability or sensitivity to lead in this type of ministry.

~ **Deliverance ministry.** This ministry actually *delivers* someone from the powers of evil and darkness that have set up strongholds in one's life. There are many different opinions about this type of ministry. Abuse and the transference of spirits, whether generational or through relationships, can give the grounds for demonic activity in someone's life. As counseling addresses these issues, freedom can be experienced. There are times when direct encounters with the powers of darkness, by the counselor and with the counselee's agreement, may be necessary.

~ Cognitive counseling, prayer ministry, and deliverance ministry work together real well in a counseling session, and they need to work together. There are aspects of a painful event that one may just need cognitive counseling. And there may be other aspects of the memory that needs prayer ministry and/or deliverance ministry.

~ In short, what you and your counselor will need to understand and deal with are any and all of the following: thoughts, beliefs, thinking patterns/strongholds, feelings/emotions, vows, judgments, soul ties/bonds, transference of and open doors for demonic activity, and behaviors. At the root of these issues, if they are negative, are the lies of the enemy. Christian bookstores sell many books on these subjects.

~ You may go back and forth in thinking about your decision to pursue counseling. One day you may want counseling; the next day you may not want it. You may feel fear. You may feel mistrust. Only you can work through your thoughts and feelings to make that decision. Hopefully, in hearing Naomi's journey, you will be encouraged to seek counseling.

~ If you decide in favor of counseling, you need to think about what would be important to you: the **type of counseling** you want to have or need to have; the type of **training** you want your counselor to have; how much **experience** you want your counselor to have; do you prefer a **same sex or opposite sex** counselor; what is their **reputation**. Think through these issues and make phone calls and ask questions.

3. **Start and/or build relationships.** Even as you just read that word, *relationships*, you may cringe because you may have been deeply hurt in a past relationship or maybe you are in a hurtful relationship while reading this book. It is certainly understandable if you fear them, not feeling safe. Yet, it is within the realm of relationships that healing can happen. Talk to God, telling Him how you feel about getting involved in relationships. May I suggest that you merely be open for God to bring people into your life with whom you can feel safe and who will walk with you as you travel this journey. This is most important.

    Having people walk with you during this journey will help you to understand the value and power of presence. Understanding and experiencing presence will help issues such as rejection and abandonment. It will also help you to understand the work and ministry of the Holy Spirit, including His presence in your life.

4. **Spend some time everyday building your relationship with the Lord.** This is critically important. Think of it as your focused time with the Lord, a time you can focus on the Lord. It involves talking to God, God talking to you, reading from the Bible, writing in a journal and/or worshipping Him through music. Start somewhere, even if it is just a few minutes each day. Christian bookstores have material that can help you.

5. **Understand and enter into a lifestyle of praise and worship.** Praise and worship are an acknowledgement and expression of what God does and who He is. They need to go outside the walls of your church and even outside your everyday focused time with the Lord. They are most necessary in your daily life, especially in light of the battle you may encounter with the enemy. Praise and worship usher in the presence of the Lord. And the presence of the Lord gives victory over the devil. As you go throughout your day, praise and worship God! You may be surprised at how the oppression and depression you experience may lift!

6. **Understand spiritual warfare.** The devil has been very happy to see you live your life driven by his lies and painful emotion. He wants you to stay in that very place. So he will do everything he can to keep you in that place of deception. But as you receive healing, you will learn how he works. Remember that his mission is to steal, kill, and destroy. His tools are the lies he can trick you to believe. He used a lie with Eve and he uses his lies with you and me. You are in a battle and you can learn how to fight and receive the victory! Please note that warfare and worship go hand in hand. It is very unwise to enter into deliberately warring against your enemy without entering into worship. Read the story in II Chronicles 20:5-23, especially noting verse 22. Christian bookstores sell many books on this subject.

7. **Learn to receive from the Lord.** As God's child, He has many blessings for you. Many blessings will be revealed to you as you read the Bible. Many are discovered in worship or prayer. However you come upon His blessings, receive them because they are rightfully yours as God's child.

8. **Consider being anointed.** Mark 6:13 teaches us that many sick people were healed through getting anointed with oil. James 5:14 and 15 gives instruction for sick people to call on the Elders of their church to pray over them in faith and anoint them with oil. This was a tremendous help to Naomi. Meditate on those verses and ask the Lord if He would have you do that.

9. **Medicine.** Do not go off any of your medicine! Do not go off any of your medicine! Do not go off any of your medicine! Medicine may be critical to your daily functioning. As healing occurs and you discuss how you are feeling with your doctor, he/she will decide how to adjust your medication. Naomi was on medicine for a time and then her doctor weaned her off.

10. **Take care of yourself.** As you go through your healing journey, there may be some extremely stressful times. It is important to take care of yourself. Eat well, get exercise, and keep regular sleeping routines. Talk with your doctor about vitamin and herbal supplements that may help to keep you healthy and strong. You may want to also consider the application of essential oils as Naomi did. Essential oils are drawn from plants. They are extremely potent and go directly into your blood stream for purposes of detoxifying and rebuilding your body. Drink eight glasses of water each day. And have your water tested for pollutants as those pollutants can cause one to become sick. Also investigate regular chiropractic adjustments and reflexology treatments as they work to keep the body in balance.

11. **Rest** in the Lord. I have suggested many things for you to do for your healing. They are critically

important and they are good. However, learning to rest in the Lord is a powerful part of your healing. Although resting implies doing nothing, rest happens when you choose to enter into the presence of God through praise and worship. As you enter into worship and praise, stay there and keep worshipping and praising. Soak it up; soak it in. In His presence, there is rest.

What God Uses

1. **His Word**—The Bible is your greatest weapon against the forces of evil. Jesus used it when the devil tempted Him in the wilderness (Matthew 4:1-11; Luke 4:1-13). Sit under people with the gift of teaching so you can learn what the Bible is saying to you. **Read** it, **meditate** on it, **memorize** it, **believe** it, **study** it, **apply** it, **speak** it out, and **teach** it. As you practice these disciplines, the Holy Spirit will give you great empowerment and anointing. The following are some wonderful and encouraging facts about God's Word:

   - The Bible **is** a . . .
     - **manual** to teach you how to keep from sin so you can live a Godly life. Psalm 119:1-3,9, 11
     - **book** full of promises that you are to believe. II Peter 1:4
     - **lamp** and **light** to your path, showing you the right way to live. Psalm 119:105,130, 133
     - **mirror** showing the **true motives** of your heart (why you do something). James 1:23-25
     - **sword** to destroy the lies of Satan that are in your mind. Ephesians 6:17
     - **hammer** that shatters the lies of Satan that are in your mind. Jeremiah 23:29

- The "**personality**" of the Bible. It . . .
  - is **pure**—real, simple, clear, spotless, without sin or sin's effects. Psalm 12:6; 19:8; 119:140; I Peter 2:2
  - is **living, active**, and **sharp**. Hebrews 4:12
  - contains words spoken by God, which are "**spirit**" and "**life**." John 6:63
  - is **profitable** and **useful**. II Timothy 3:16-17

- What the Bible **does**. It . . .
  - works **in** you! I Thessalonians 2:13
  - **births** you into the family of God. James 1:18,21; I Peter 1:23
  - **cleanses** you. Psalm 119:9; Ephesians 5:25-26; John 15:3
  - makes **faith** start and grow in you. Romans 10:17
  - brings **joy**. Psalm 119:111; I John 1:4
  - gives **peace** to those who love it. Psalm 119:165
  - gives **hope**. Psalm 119:49; 130:5; Jeremiah 29:11; Romans 15:4
  - **heals** you. Psalm 107:20
  - brings **deliverance**. Psalm 119:170
  - gives **freedom**. John 8:31-32; John 17:17
  - **keeps you from being swallowed up** in the midst of your hurts. Psalm 119:92-93
  - brings **wisdom, insight**, and **understanding** to hard situations. Psalm 119:98-99, 104,130
  - brings **stability** and **strength**. Psalm 1:2,3; 119:28
  - gives **energy** or **revives** or **enriches life**. Psalm 119:14,25,50,72,127,162
  - **renews** your mind. Romans 12:2; Ephesians 4:17-23
  - **guides** you, **watches** over you, and **talks** to you (through the Holy Spirit who lives in-

side). Proverbs 6:20-22
- **judges** the **thoughts** and **intentions** of the heart. Hebrews 4:12
- **teaches**, **reproves** (points out wrong behavior with person feeling conviction), **corrects**, and **trains** you how to do the right thing, making you **adequate** and **equipped** for every good work. II Timothy 3:16-17
- is **not bound**, meaning that man cannot hold back its work in someone's life. II Timothy 2:9
- **chases the enemy** as it is spoken out loud. Matthew 4:1-11; Luke 4:1-13

2. **Holy Spirit**—There are differing views about the role of the Holy Spirit in one's life. However, the following are some basic truths to know and understand:
   - The Holy Spirit is the Spirit of God and the Spirit of Jesus.
   - As you are encountering pain, be aware of, acknowledge, and fellowship with the presence of the Holy Spirit as He is right there with you in your pain. That fellowship has a way of bringing peace.
   - The Holy Spirit is to be your ultimate Guide. Yes, teachers and counselors are certainly needed, but they give their own Holy Spirit interpretation concerning situations. Learn to listen to and comprehend what counselors and teachers are saying to you. Then ask the Holy Spirit for direction and guidance. Maybe the counsel of the Holy Spirit will be what your counselors and teachers tell you to do, but maybe it will be something different.
   - The Holy Spirit gives revelation. Revelation is an uncovering or unveiling of something hidden. If you are open to the Holy Spirit, He will bring

powerful revelation about you and your situation, all to help you heal and receive victory.

- God's desire is that you would become fully controlled by the Holy Spirit, living in and through His total anointing.

3. **Prayer**—Here are some simple and helpful points to understand concerning prayer.

- Although there is much we can learn about prayer, it is merely you talking to God and God talking to you. It is about relationship. It is about His presence. Talk with Him as you would talk with a friend.

- The book of Psalms explodes with the reality of life. We see cries, praises, pain, frustrations, questions, joy, asking for needs to be met, humble confessions, and worship.

- God absolutely responds to prayer. It may not be in the way you want at that time, but you can be sure that God acts on your prayer (Numbers 14:11-20; James 5:16). Absolutely expect an answer, knowing it will be done according to God's way and in His timing!

- Prayer is saying, "I can't God, but you can." If you are not praying, you are saying that you do not need God.

- Praying continually as I Thessalonians 5:17 says, is living in an attitude of prayer, a continual state of depending on God for direction, wisdom, insight, discernment, and more.

- As you encounter certain difficulties in your life and healing journey and in the lives of those you love, you can learn how to pray effectively. Christian bookstores sell many books that can teach and instruct you in this area.

- May I suggest that you investigate the following topics concerning prayer: praying in the name of Jesus; praying the blood of Jesus; praying through the binding and loosing prin-

ciples; praying in tongues; praying in the authority you have as God's child; praying the promises of God; praying intercessory prayer.
- Yes, prayer is work, but it is so exciting and powerful.

4. **Faith**—Expect God to heal you, mentally, emotionally, physically, and spiritually, until He does differently. Realize that some healing may not come until you reach heaven's doors.
- He does not always heal, but believe Him for it as we are to walk a walk of faith (Habakkuk 2:4; Romans 1:17; Galatians 3:11; Colossians 2:6,7; Hebrews 10:38).
- He may give instantaneous healing and He may not.
- Jesus could do no miracles in his hometown because of the unbelief of the people (Matthew 13:58). And Jesus refers to a multitude of people as an "unbelieving generation," the reason for a boy's lack of healing (Matthew 17:17; Mark 9:19; Luke 9:41). I wonder how healthy God's church would be if, as a 100% whole across this globe, the church, no matter what the denomination, would together believe God for instantaneous healing in situations. I think the unbelief within the church hinders God's healing.

In a Nutshell . . .

1. You can **know about** God. And you can even **follow** Jesus. But you may not **know** God and the presence of His Spirit in a personal way. Yes, knowledge about God and following Jesus can bring freedom and peace in your life. However, God wants you to **experience** what you know. For example, you probably **know** that God loves you, but have you **experienced** that love? And you

probably **know** that the Holy Spirit lives in you, but have you **encountered** that life-changing presence? We have a God who wants you to experience and encounter Him and His life-changing attributes. We certainly experience sin with all of its dark and deadly emotion. Why not experience the powerful presence of the Holy Spirit and all His fruit?

2. Pressing in for your healing will open the doors for you to experience the Holy Spirit's presence and fruit in a powerful and life-changing way. It will move you into great spiritual growth.

3. And, most important is that in experiencing the sweet presence of the Holy Spirit, you will experience rest.

Because God loves you, He acted in a most outrageous way to bring you, yes you, out of the pain of sin and into a relationship with Him. In bringing you out of that pain, you will need to deal with your human feelings and emotions. God created feelings and emotion and wants you to not only understand them, but He wants you to know how to deal with them. God desperately desires that you live a life where peace daily rules your heart, joy overflows the boring tasks of each day, and you experience contentment, all because you know the presence and flow of the Holy Spirit within you in a personal way. The resources in Appendix II are there to help you as you travel this journey of healing.

If you are willing to learn how to understand and deal with your feelings and emotions in a healthy way, your jagged-edged pebbles will become smooth. As they become smooth, the pebbles will become smaller. When they are smaller, the pile of pebbles will shift, moving your mountain. With that mountain moved, you will be able to clearly see and come to personally know God, Jesus Christ, and the Holy Spirit like never before.

God is pursuing you, running after you, as He did to Adam and Eve, as He did to Naomi. Naomi asked an important question in the beginning of this book, "Are you willing to travel the journey of healing God has for you?"

Now I ask you, too. "Are you willing?"

My People, My Culture

My name is Naomi Stoltzfus. I had this book written primarily for my people, the Old Order Amish. I do, however, know and deeply hope that people of other Amish groups, Mennonite groups, and even those within the English culture will read this book.

I love my people and culture. I wanted to have the opportunity to briefly explain the Old Order Amish church and culture for those who do not know or understand how we live. However, as you read this section, it is extremely important for you to under-stand that the Amish way of life can vary. What I have written, therefore, is based only on **my** life experi-ence within the Old Order Amish from the time I was a child up to the present time.

In 1525 during the Protestant Reformation in Europe the Anabaptist movement began over the issue of water baptism. Those in that movement desired to live by the simple faith and practice as seen in the early Christian church which is taught in the Bible. In time, Menno Simons came to the movement and began the Mennonite denomination. In time, a gentleman, Jacob Ammon, thought the Mennonite denomination was changing too rapidly. He did, there-fore, break away and start the Amish culture, in order to live plain. Over the years since then there have been many divisions and break-offs from each group. Each group lives by different rules.

In considering my group, the Old Order Amish, what is the shortest description I can give about us?

We are families working hard together and finding great fulfillment in carrying out our work. We do not want idle time as idle time can get one in trouble. We believe in family and that families should be like teams, working hard together to keep their farm or business operating well.

For children, chores are to be done before and after school. Only on rare occasions do children receive allowances for doing chores because hard work is a natural and expected way of life.

We live and dress very plain and alike because, as individuals, we do not want to bring attention to ourselves. We live without electricity. Our telephones are outside. We do not own cars, but we will pay someone to take us somewhere if it is too far for our horse and buggy or if time is an issue. We call a person who drives us to places, our driver. We can also travel by train or boat. We do not travel by plane. It is against the rules of the church to have your picture taken because Exodus 20:4 says, "You shall not make for yourself an idol, or any likeness of what is in heaven above or on the earth, beneath or in the water under the earth."

Our schools are one room, with all ages learning in the same classroom. The teacher has the challenge of teaching all ages in that one room. We finish school at the eighth grade and do not go to college. After school we work at a job or at our home or somewhere else.

We do not build church buildings because church services, weddings, and funerals are held in homes. The money we give at church is used to help each other for any extraordinary needs, like medical bills, since we do not invest in health insurance. We strongly believe in helping one another. If someone needs a barn built, we all help. When help is needed during a crisis, wedding, or funeral, we are immediately there for each other.

Weddings are usually in November, always on either a Tuesday or a Thursday so it is a very busy time of the year. Mondays and Wednesdays are the days of preparation. It is a time when everyone in the bride's family helps. Weddings are usually held in the home of the bride. There are times when a family may have to build a hall just for the wedding day in order to accommodate all the people. It is taken down when the wedding is over. On the day of the wedding, the parents are treated as a king and queen, with no work responsibilities. Friends and church members do all the work.

In the days when David and I were married, newlyweds spent the wedding night in the home where they were married. The next morning the newlyweds helped to clean up the wedding mess. They also spent Sunday night together. Then a different routine set in. From Monday to Friday, the bride lived with her family and the groom lived with his family. They only spent the weekend together at the bride's home. This routine was followed until the spring when they moved into their own home.

However, it is different today. After the wedding, the husband moves in with the wife's parents. They live there until the spring when they move into their own home.

On weekends, over the Christmas holidays and throughout the winter months after the wedding, the newlyweds visit friends and receive their wedding gifts.

Women and men in other cultures wear wedding rings as a statement that they are married. However, our men grow a beard as their statement of marriage. Women wear no ring, like English women, to indicate that they are married.

Before the couple moves into their home together, they can choose to go on a honeymoon. Not all couples make that choice. It can be anytime after the wedding and before they move in together.

The youngest male child usually takes over the farm or business. When that happens, the parents build a home on the property for themselves or they build an addition to the house.

When someone passes away, their body is viewed in the home of the one who passed away and the service is held right there in the home. Neighbors come immediately after the death to help organize the house for all the people who will visit. If someone passes away in their own home or on their own property, the funeral director then comes and picks up the body and returns it within about four hours, ready for viewing and burial. The viewing is continuous from the time the funeral director returns the body until the actual funeral service. People can come at any time to view the body. Benches, which are in a big gray box on wheels, are transported on a horse-drawn carriage to the house in order to accommodate seating for everyone. The minister of the church performs the ceremony.

Within each state, the Amish church is divided into geographical districts. And within each district is one church. The church is made up of people who live in that district. A bishop is assigned to each district for the purpose of overseeing the church within that district. However, at times a bishop may oversee more than one district. Only the bishop can perform marriage ceremonies, baptisms, and membership classes. The bishop also determines the church policies, rules, and discipline structure for that district. Each church has two ministers who lead the Sunday preaching and one deacon who reads the New Testament reading during the church service. He also assists in baptisms. The deacon works with the two ministers.

Church services are held every other week at members' homes on a rotation basis. Because there are about 25 families in each church, a family hosts church about once a year. The services are either held in the family's barn or in the shop of their business or right in their home if it is big enough. The benches, as mentioned above, which are in the big gray box on wheels, are transported from house to house between the services.

Church services start at 8:00 a.m. and continue until 11:30 a.m. A meal prepared by the host family is then shared with everyone. The afternoon is spent visiting with each other. On the Sundays that there is no church, each family is supposed to have devotions together in the morning, while the afternoons and evenings are spent visiting friends and family.

The bishop determines the rules for each district. Breaking any of the rules can cause one to be under church discipline which has different levels.

Joining church is a big commitment because it is the time when one moves from childhood into adulthood while giving up their own personal desires in order to follow the church for the rest of their life. It requires attending nine instruction classes. Each class is held for one-half hour during the singing time at church. During those classes one learns about Adam and Eve, other Old Testament stories, Jesus' birth, death, and resurrection, and the rules of the church. After those nine weeks are over, one is to confess Jesus as their Lord and Savior and make a commitment to stay with the church. A baptism service is what actually makes one a church member. The day before one is baptized, there is a special gathering of parents, grandparents, and those getting baptized. It is a time when the leaders of the church explain the foundation of our beliefs. Then a meal is served.

There are no other church or church-oriented services other than a Sunday service every other week. The church does, however, have youth groups so the youth have a place to socialize. The youth groups have hymn sings and other activities such as volleyball. This group allows the youth to learn to know other youth. It is usually where the youth find their mate. One thing I have learned over the years is that just like the English culture, there is plenty of misconduct with our youth. There is alcohol and drug abuse and wrong sexual activity.

We can become a member of church between the ages of 15 and 16 as the opportunity to join only comes every other year. However, boys often do not become members until the age of 19 or 20. From the age of 16 on, our teens have the option of participating in *Rumspringa*. This is a time when teens can participate in English culture activities and ways of life to determine if they want to stay or leave the Old Order Amish church. It is solely their choice to participate. Some teens actually leave their home and live somewhere else. If they leave, they will be shunned from their families. That means they will not be included in all the family activities. If they decide to stay, they are to join church and submit to the ways and rules of the church.

Our culture is a quiet culture, mostly staying to ourselves, yet helping each other very much whenever help is needed. We deny ourselves the pleasures of life and society. Even though we hold to strong values, we struggle with sin as much as people within any other culture.

We call white Americans, English.

Although my husband I have relationships with other people in other cultures, we are happy to be where God wants us within the Old Order Amish.

Appendix II

Recommended Reading

We have listed books below that can help you in your journey of healing. The list includes many authors with a wide variety of belief concerning how God works today. There are many more books available in Christian bookstores. Books are a great source to help, but make sure you do not neglect to read the book with life-giving words of the Holy Spirit, the Bible.

Allender, Dr. Dan B., *The Wounded Heart (Colorado Springs, Colo.:* NavPress, 1990).

_____, *The Healing Path* (Colorado Springs, Colo.: Waterbrook Press, 1999).

Allender, Dr. Dan B. and Dr. Tremper Longman, III, *The Cry of the Soul, How our Emotions Reveal our Deepest Questions About God* (Colorado Springs, Colo.: NavPress Publishing Group, 1994).

Anderson, Neil T., *The Bondage Breaker, Overcoming Negative Thoughts, Irrational Feelings and Habitual Sin* (Eugene, Ore.: Harvest House Publishers, 1993).

_____. *Living Free in Christ, The Truth About Who You Are and How Christ Can Meet Your Deepest Needs (Ventura, Calif.:* Regal, a division of Gospel Light, 1993).

_____. *Victory Over the Darkness, Realizing the Power of Your Identity in Christ* (Ventura, Calif.: Regal Books, a Division of Gospel Light, 1990).

_____. *Walking in the Light, Discerning God's Guidance in an Age of Spiritual Counterfeit* (Nashville, Tenn.: Thomas Nelson Publishers, 1992).

Anderson, Neil T. and Rich Miller, *Walking in Freedom, A 21-day Devotional to Help Establish Your Freedom in Christ* (Ventura, Calif.: Regal Books, a division of Gospel Light, 1999).

Bateman, Lana L., *Bible Promises for the Healing Journey* (Westwood, N.J.: Barbour and Company, Inc., 1991).

Bennett, Dennis, *How to Pray for the Release of the Holy Spirit, What the Baptism of the Holy Spirit is and How to Pray for It* (Gainesville, Fla.: Bridge-Logos, 1985).

Bennett, Dennis and Rita, *The Holy Spirit and You (North Brunswick, N.J.:* Bridge-Logos Publishers, 1971).

Bevere, John, *Thus Saith the Lord, How to Know When God Is Speaking to You Through Another* (Lake Mary, Fla.: Charisma House, a Strang Company, 1999).

Bounds, E.M., *Power Through Prayer* (Chicago, Ill.: Moody Press, 1979).

Bubeck, Mark I., *The Adversary, the Christian Versus Demon Activity* (Chicago, Ill.: Moody Press, 1975).

_____, *Overcoming the Adversary, Warfare Praying Against Demon Activity* (Chicago, Ill.: Moody Press, 1984).

Cherry, Reginald, M.D., *Healing Prayer, God's Divine Intervention in Medicine, Faith, and Prayer* (Carmel, N.Y.: Guideposts, 1999).

Deere, Jack, *Surprised by the Power of the Spirit* (Grand Rapids, Mich.: Zondervan Publishing House, 1993).

_____, *Surprised by the Voice of God* (Grand Rapids, Mich.: Zondervan Publishing House, 1996).

DeMoss, Nancy, *Lies Women Believe, and the Truth that Sets Them Free* (Chicago, Ill.: Moody Press, 2001).

Frangipane, Francis, *The Three Battlegrounds, An In-depth View of the Three Arenas of Spiritual Warfare: The Mind, the Church, and the Heavenly Places* (Cedar Rapids, Ia.: Arrow Publications, 1989).

Good, Meryl and Phyllis, *20 Most Asked Questions About the Amish and Mennonite* (Intercourse, Pa.: Good Books, 1979).

Gothard, Bill, *The Power of Crying Out, When Prayer Becomes Mighty* (Sisters, Ore.: Multonomah Publishers, 2002).

Guyon, Madame, *Experiencing God Through Prayer* (Springdale, Pa.: Whitaker House, 1984).

Hammond, Lynne and Patsy Cameneti, *Secrets to Powerful Prayer* (Tulsa, Okla.: Harrison House, 2000).

Hayford, Jack, *The Beauty of Spiritual Language, Unveiling the Ministry of Speaking in Tongues* (Nashville, Tenn.: Thomas Nelson Publishers, 1996).

Heggen, Carolyn Holderread, *Sexual Abuse in Christian Homes and Churches* (Scottdale, Pa.: Herald Press, 1993).

Hinn, Benny, *The Anointing* (Nashville, Tenn.: Thomas Nelson Publishers, 1992).

_____, *The Blood, Experience Its Power to Transform You* (Lake Mary, Fla.: Charisma House, a Strang Company, 2001).

_____, *Good Morning, Holy Spirit* (Nashville, Tenn.: Thomas Nelson Publishers, 1990).

Jakes, T.D., *The Lady, Her Lover, and Her Lord* (N.Y.: Berkley Books, 1998).

_____, *Woman, Thou Art Loosed, Healing the Wounds of the Past* (Shippensburg, Pa.: Treasure House, an imprint of Destiny Image Publishers, Inc., 1993).

Kendall, R.T., *Total Forgiveness, When Everything in You Wants to Hold a Grudge, Point a Finger and Remember the Pain, God Wants You to Lay It All Aside* (Lake Mary, Fla.: Charisma House, a part of Strang Communications Co., 2002).

Kroeger, Catherine Clark and James R. Beck, *Woman, Abuse and the Bible, How Scripture Can be Used to Hurt or Heal* (Grand Rapids, Mich.: Baker Books, 1996).

Kuhlman, Kathryn, *The Greatest Power in the World* (North Brunswick, N.J.: Bridge-Logos Publishers, 1997).

Langberg, Diane Mandt, Ph.D., *On the Threshold of Hope, Opening the Door to Healing For Survivors of Sexual Abuse* (Wheaton, Ill.: Tyndale House Publishers, Inc., 1999).

Lutzer, Erwin W., *The Serpent of Paradise, The Incredible Story of How Satan's Rebellion Serves God's Purposes* (Chicago, Ill.: Moody Press, 1996).

Manning, Brennan, *The Ragamuffin Gospel, Embracing the Unconditional Love of God* (Sisters, Ore.: Multnomah Books, 1990).

Matzat, Don, *Christ Esteem, Where the Search for Self-esteem Ends* (Eugene, Ore.: Harvest House Publishers, 1990).

McGee, Robert S., *The Search for Significance* (Nashville, Tenn.: W Publishing Group, a division of Thomas Nelson, Inc., 2003).

Meyers, Joyce, *Managing Your Emotions, Instead of Your Emotions Managing You* (Tulsa, Okla.: Harrison House, 1973).

_____, *The Battlefield of the Mind, Winning the Battle in Your Mind* (Tulsa, Okla.: Harrison House, 1995).

Murry, Andrew, *The Prayer Life* (Grand Rapids, Mich.: Zondervan Publishing House, 1968).

Omartian, Stormie, *Lord, I Want to Be Whole* (Nashville, Tenn.: Thomas Nelson Publishers, 2000).

Ortberg, John, *Love Beyond Reason* (Grand Rapids, Mich.: Zondervan Publishing House, 1998).

Paxson, Ruth, *The Work of God the Holy Spirit* (Chicago, Ill.: Moody Press, 1958).

Pierce, Chuck D., *Prayers that Outwit the Enemy* (Ventura, Calif.: Regal Books, 2004).

Prince, Derek, *Blessing or Curse, Freedom From Pressures You Thought You Had to Live With* (Grand Rapids, Mich., Chosen Books, a division of Baker Book House Co., 1990).

Sandford, John and Mark, *A Comprehensive Guide to Deliverance and Inner Healing* (Grand Rapids, Mich., Chosen Books, a Division of Baker Book House Co., 1992).

Sandford, John and Paula, *The Transformation of the Inner Man, The Most Comprehensive Book on Inner Healing Today* (Tulsa, Okla.: Victory House, Inc., 1982).

_____, *Healing the Wounded Spirit* (Tulsa, Okla.: Victory House, Inc., 1985).

Savard, Liberty S., *Breaking the Power, of Unmet Needs, of Unhealed Hurts, Unresolved Issues in Your Life* (North Brunswick, N.J.: Bridge-Logos Publishers, 1997).

_____, *Shattering Your Strongholds, Freedom From Your Struggles* (North Brunswick, N.J.: Bridge-Logos Publishers, 1992).

_____, *Unsurrendered Soul, Are You Ready to Surrender Yours?* (Gainesville, Fla.: Bridge-Logos, 2002).

Schaumburg, Dr. Harry W., *False Intimacy* (Colorado Springs, Colo.: NavPress, 1993).

Seamands, David, *Healing of Memories* (Wheaton, Ill.: Victor Books, a division of SP Publications, 1985).

_____, *Healing for Damaged Emotions* (Wheaton, Ill.: Victor Books, a division of SP Publications, Inc., 1981).

_____, *Succeeding in Enemy Territory* (Mansfield, Pa.: Kingdom Publishing, 1990).

Sheets, Dutch, *Intercessory Prayer, How God Can Use Your Prayers to Move Heaven and Earth* (Ventura, Calif.: Regal Books, a division of Gospel Light, 1996).

Sherrer, Quin, *Miracles Happen When You Pray* (Grand Rapids, Mich.: Zondervan Publishing House, 1997).

Smith, Hannah Whiteall, *The Christian's Secret of a Happy Life* (Grand Rapids, Mich.: Fleming H. Revell, a division of Baker Book House Company, 1952).

Stanley, Charles, *Forgiveness* (Nashville, Tenn.: Oliver Nelson, a division of Thomas Nelson Publishers, 1987).

_____, *How to Listen to God* (Nashville, Tenn.: Oliver Nelson, a division of Thomas Nelson Publishers, 1985).

_____, *The Wonderful Spirit-Filled Life* (Nashville, Tenn.: Oliver Nelson, a division of Thomas Nelson Publishers, 1992).

Torrey, R.A., *How to Pray* (Chicago, Ill.: Moody Press).

Unger, Merrill, *What Demons Can Do to Saints* (Chicago, Ill.: Moody Press, 1977).

Vernick, Leslie, *The Truth Principle, A Life-changing Model for Spiritual Growth and Renewal* (Colorado Springs, Colo.: Waterbrook Press, 2000).

Vines Expository Dictionary of Old and New Testament Words.

Waltman, Dawn Siegrist, *A Rose in Heaven, A Journey of Hope and Healing for Women who Grieve the Loss of Their Baby* (Paradise, Pa.: Paradise Publications, 1999).

Warren, Rick, *The Purpose Driven Life, What on Earth Am I Here For?* (Grand Rapids, Mich.: Zondervan, 2002).

Wigglesworth, Smith, Any and all of his books.

Wright, Henry W., *A More Excellent Way, A Teaching on the Spiritual Roots of Disease* (Thomaston, Calif.: Pleasant Valley Publications, a Division of Pleasant Valley Church, Inc., 2002).

RESOURCES

Wellspring Garden Ministries thanks you for taking the time to read this book. The Wellspring Garden Ministries Center was opened in January 2001 with the desire to walk alongside women as they travel their healing journey. This is accomplished through counseling, discipling, and mentoring.

We invite you to contact us through the information provided below:

Wellspring Garden Ministries
5207 Old Philadelphia Pike
P.O. Box 236
Kinzers, PA 17535
717-768-7546
E-mail: hope@wellspringgarden.org
Web site: www.wellspringgarden.org

COUNSELING and TRAINING

We invite those who live in the Lancaster County area to contact any of the ministry/counseling centers listed below in order to receive the help and/or training needed. We suggest you telephone or email the centers, asking questions to determine if that specific ministry/counseling center would be beneficial for you. (All resources have granted permission to be listed.)

Abundant Living Ministries
541 W. 28th Division Highway
Lititz, PA
717-626-9575
E-mail: abunliv@juno.com

Breath of Life Ministries
70 Clay School Road
Ephrata, PA 17522
717-733-8751
E-mail: bolm7@hotmail.com

Freedom Ministry
133 E. Vine Street
Lancaster, PA 17602
717-299-0667

Life Ministries
250 Meadow Lane
Conestoga, PA 17516
717-871-0540
E-mail: nmartin@life-ministries.com

Petra Christian Fellowship
565 Airport Road
New Holland, PA 17557
717-354-5394
E-mail: info@petrafel.org
Web site: www.petrafel.org

REST Ministries
c/o: Education/Training Department
203 N. 2nd Street
Darby, PA 19023
610-534-2686
E-mail: jedinger@rest-min.org
Web site: www.rest-min.org
(Offers training in developing support group ministries)

Samaritan Counseling Center
1803 Oregon Pike
Lancaster, PA 17601
717-560-9969
E-mail: lcrockett@scclanc.org
Web site: www.scclanc.org

Shepherd's Touch Counseling Ministries
2384 New Holland Pike
Lancaster, PA 17601
717-656-4834
Email: shepherdstouch@frontiernet.net

Spirit and Word Ministries
P.O. Box 304
Lititz, PA 17543
(Offers teaching on the effects of trauma and training in healing prayer)

Upward Call Counseling, Inc.
150 E. Franklin Street
New Holland, PA 17557
717-355-2117
E-mail: bobweaver@upwardcall.org
Web site: www.upwardcall.org

INFORMATION CONCERNING ABUSE

If you would like more specific information about abuse, we suggest that you contact any of the organizations listed below. (All resources have granted permission to be listed.)

Childhelp USA
15757 N. 78th Street
Scottsdale, AZ 85260
480-922-8212
1-800-4-A-CHILD
Web site: www.childhelpusa.org

The National Center for Victims of Crime
2000 M Street, NW
Suite 480
Washington, D.C. 20036
202-467-8700
Hotline: 1-800-394-2255
Email: gethelp@ncvc.org
Web site: www.ncvc.org

National Sexual Violence Resource Center (NSVRC)
123 North Enola Drive
Enola, PA 17025
717-728-9740
E-mail: resources@NSVRC.org
Web site: www.nsvrc.org

Pennsylvania Coalition Against Domestic Violence
6400 Flank Drive
Suite 1300
Harrisburg, PA 17112
1-800-932-4632
Web site: www.pcadv.org

Pennsylvania Coalition Against Rape
125 N. Enola Drive
Enola, PA 17025
1-717-728-9740
1-800-692-7445
E-mail: stop@PCAR.org
Web site: www.pcar.org